HOLDING ON WHEN YOU WANT TO LET GO

HOLDING ON WHEN YOU WANT TO LET GO

STUDY GUIDE

Clinging to Hope
When Life Is Falling Apart

SHEILA WALSH

BakerBooks
a division of Baker Publishing Group
Grand Rapids, Michigan

Published by Baker Books
a division of Baker Publishing Group
PO Box 6287, Grand Rapids, MI 49516-6287
www.bakerbooks.com

Printed in the United States of America

ISBN: 978-1-5409-0183-5

Study guide written by Jerusha Clark with additional material by Sheila Walsh.

Based on and with material from *Holding On When You Want to Let Go* by Sheila Walsh.

The author is represented by Dupree Miller and Associates, a global literary agency. www.dupreemiller.com

Baker Publishing Group publications use paper produced from sustainable forestry practices and post-consumer waste whenever possible.

21 22 23 24 25 26 27   7 6 5 4 3 2 1

Contents

SESSION 1 • Holding On When Life Feels Out of Control   7

SESSION 2 • Holding On When You Feel Alone and God Is Silent   19

SESSION 3 • Holding On When You're Afraid   31

SESSION 4 • Holding On When You've Messed Up   43

SESSION 5 • Held by the Promises of God   55

SESSION 6 • Held by the God Who Rescues   67

SESSION 7 • Held by the God of Miracles Who Changes Everything   79

SESSION 8 • Let Go! You Are Being Held   91

Notes   103

Holding On When Life Feels Out of Control

I feel so passionately about the message of this book. Life does not give us a quick fix, but God is always moving, always working. I see this now in ways I've never understood before. . . . I have a six-word story now, and it became this book. *Hold on and don't let go.*

Sheila Walsh

And I am convinced that nothing can ever separate us from God's love. Neither death nor life, neither angels nor demons, neither our fears for today nor our worries about tomorrow—not even the powers of hell can separate us from God's love. No power in the sky above or in the earth below—indeed, nothing in all creation will ever be able to separate us from the love of God that is revealed in Christ Jesus our Lord.

Romans 8:38-39

AS WE BEGIN THIS STUDY TOGETHER, let me ask you a question: Has your life turned out the way you thought it would?

If you're anything like me, your answer is a resounding, "No!"

When I was twenty-one or even thirty-one years old, if someone had read me the script of what would come my way, I might very well have run for the hills or buried my head in the sand (and those would have been the reasonable options!).

Life has a habit of surprising us, doesn't it? And sometimes of knocking us flat on our backs. Considering the staggering unpredictability of life makes me grateful that, as the apostle Paul wrote, "Our great power is from God, not from ourselves. We are pressed on every side by troubles, but we are not crushed. We are perplexed, but not driven to despair. We are hunted down, but never abandoned by God. We get knocked down, but we are not destroyed" (2 Cor. 4:7–9).

Don't miss this:

Pressed but not crushed . . .

Perplexed but not driven to despair . . .

Hunted down but never abandoned . . .

Knocked down but not destroyed . . .

I believe this with all my heart. In Christ, we are more than conquerors; Romans 8:37 promises this. To be perfectly frank, however, there are days I feel more like the conquered than the conqueror. Can you relate?

If so, I invite you to journey deeper into the truths you read in *Holding On When You Want to Let Go*. In this companion guide, we'll walk together, looking more intently at what God has to say and taking time to connect with Him in study, worship, and prayer.

You may recall that at the end of each chapter in the book, I included three ways to hold on to hope. Every session of this study guide will take you deeper into these sets of key principles. Right now I'd like to reintroduce you to the truths you learned in chapter 1, "Holding On When Life Feels Out of Control":

1. We were not made to do life on our own; we need to let people into our stories.
2. Jesus is still writing your story, and He holds all the pieces.
3. No matter how things appear, God is in control.

I'm eager to begin, so let's link arms and dive into our first truth.

It Is Not Good to Be Alone

When you look back on the year 2020, what do you remember? Masks? Social distancing? Protests and riots?

For many people, 2020 and the COVID-19 pandemic became synonymous with profound loneliness. Some of us were isolated from our friends at church, work, or school; others were separated from their dearest loved ones. However isolated you felt, the pandemic experience brought to light a biblical principle that God highlighted several millennia ago: "It is not good for the man to be alone" (Gen. 2:18).

This stunning proclamation came after God had created a glorious world of sea, land, and sky, all teeming with life. With the advent of stars and planets, dragonflies and dolphins, God pronounced, "It is good." And it was.

Then the Lord made man in His own image, filling Adam with dignity and divine purpose. Adam enjoyed unbroken fellowship with God in the garden He had designed. What could possibly be wrong with this picture? Our Lord identified only one thing as "not good": isolation.

The man was not meant to be alone. And neither were you.

TRUTH #1: We were not made to do life on our own; we need to let people into our stories.

How do you respond to this truth? What thoughts or memories does it bring up for you? Take a moment to ask the Holy Spirit to reveal how you feel about needing others, then write your response in the space below.

In *Holding On When You Want to Let Go*, I shared a bit of my own pandemic experience with you. It was a difficult time for me, with thirty canceled speaking engagements, the financial insecurity those cancellations created, being separated from my son when he contracted the coronavirus, and the weight of anxiety that increased as the year dragged on. I also wrote about my journey *out* of that place. I discovered anew, as the verse with which I opened this session declares, that nothing can separate me from the love of God. *Nothing.*

I also relearned why God gave us so many "one another" statements in the Bible.

Pray for one another . . .

Love one another . . .

Bear one another's burdens . . .

We need one another . . . desperately! As I wrote in chapter 1, "I know now in a way I've never understood before that when our hearts are broken, we need to be able to say it out loud. If we don't, we sink deeper and deeper into the pit. We need each other. We need to let people into our pain when it is too much to carry by ourselves."[1]

Is it easy or difficult for you to let people into your pain? Why?

_____

_____

If it is difficult for you to let people in, turn your answer into a prayer of confession. Then ask the Lord to move you toward healing and hope. If allowing people in is easy for you, turn your answer into a prayer of gratitude and lift up your brothers and sisters who struggle in this area. Use the space below (and the margins too, if you need them!). Prayer—for ourselves and for others—is one of the main ways we hold on to Jesus in hope.

_____

_____

_____

Lay Your Burdens Down

In Galatians 6:2, God commands, "Bear one another's burdens, and so fulfill the law of Christ" (ESV). As you may remember, the Greek word used here for "burden" (*baros*) literally means "a heavy weight or stone someone is required to carry for a long distance."

Can't you just *feel* it? The weight of unexpected sickness. The weight of uninvited sorrow. The weight of unresolved conflict. The weight of secret shame. God did not design us to carry these burdens by ourselves.

It's quite rare to experience a season with no burdens. If that's where you are today, I rejoice with you. If, however, you are carrying a heavy load, I'd like to offer you the chance to put it down. "Cast all your anxiety on him because he cares for you," 1 Peter 5:7 (NIV) affirms.

In the space below, unburden yourself to the Lord. Use as many or as few words as you need to lay your burden in the arms of your loving Savior, Jesus.

_____

_____

_____

I love the Word of God. It has literally saved my life, so when I study it, I love to dig deep using various translations. That's not as hard as you might imagine. I use my English Standard Version Study Bible for the helpful notes. I love the readability of the New Living Translation. And I also enjoy The Message, which renders biblical language in such beautiful, accessible ways. For example, take a moment to read this well-known passage from Matthew as written in The Message:

> Are you tired? Worn out? . . . Come to me. Get away with me and you'll recover your life. I'll show you how to take a real rest. Walk with me and work with me—watch how I do it. Learn the unforced rhythms of grace. I won't lay anything heavy or ill-fitting on you. Keep company with me and you'll learn to live freely and lightly. (11:28–30)

How might your life be different if you kept company with God, learning to live freely and lightly in the unforced rhythms of grace?

_____

_____

_____

Now that we've had an opportunity to unburden ourselves to Jesus, let's return to the words of Galatians 6:2, which command us to help carry one another's troubles.

Let me ask you a personal question: Have you ever considered that this verse implies not only that we must help bear the burdens of others but also that we must allow others to help bear our burdens? How do you respond to this?

_____

_____

_____

During a group counseling session, I was once asked to use modeling clay to tell part of my story. I resisted at first (let's just say I don't have a natural affinity for sculpting), but being the obedient girl I am, I eventually gave in and started molding. When I was done, I discovered that I had made a little girl with abnormally long arms surrounded by a high wall. Without intending to, I had made a representation of an unspoken belief I carried at that time: I am available to help anyone else, but no one can get close to help me. I'm confident that God, my perfect Father, looked down on the loneliness of my heart and proclaimed, "It is not good for Sheila to be alone." It is not good for you to be alone either.

Dear friend, take a moment to ask the Holy Spirit to bring to mind one person with whom you can share the burden you currently carry. Write his or her name in the space below.

_____

Now, here's the potentially scary part. As we close this section of our study guide, send a text or make a call, inviting that person to take a walk or share a cup of tea (which, by the way, is the Scottish remedy for everything from hangnails to heartache) with you. Share any burden you are carrying with the person God brought to your mind.

Reaching out for prayer, letting others know we are hurting, and even asking for help can feel humbling. Scratch that. It *is* humbling. Praise God we have a Savior who humbled Himself and became vulnerable for our sake. Remember what Paul said about Christ:

> Though he was God,
> > he did not think of equality with God
> > as something to cling to.
> Instead, he gave up his divine privileges;
> > he took the humble position of a slave
> > and was born as a human being.
> When he appeared in human form,
> > he humbled himself in obedience to God
> > and died a criminal's death on a cross. (Phil. 2:6–8)

Jesus set the perfect example of humility. He's inviting you to experience the freedom and power of laying down your pride, your fear, your shame. Today is the day to embrace this truth: you were not made to do life on your own; you need to let people into your story.

Unfinished

The world is divided into two groups of people: those who like jigsaw puzzles and those who see them as a form of extended torture. I just happen to belong to the first group. There's something about puzzles that helps the disorderliness of my life feel less chaotic. Some years ago, I received a magnificent lion puzzle as a gift and spent a good deal of time putting the pieces together. Things were going splendidly . . . until they weren't.

If your stomach is clenching with secondhand anxiety, you may know what's coming. One piece was missing. And it wasn't the kind of piece you could shrug off with an "Oh well, life is like that" attitude. For goodness' sake, the piece contained one of the lion's eyes! For one shining moment, the idea of creating an eye patch for my lion puzzle didn't seem too bizarre.

Despite my best efforts and a whole-house cleaning, I simply could not find that piece. Imagine my shock and awe when, *two years later*, I found the mangled puzzle piece buried inside my dog's toy basket. Even though I now had the piece, I was not able to fit it together with the rest of the puzzle.

I don't know many people who like incomplete or unfinished things.

When it comes to the adventure of faith, however, the word *unfinished* takes on an entirely different meaning. As one scholar described it, "The unfinished quality of our lives is a blessing. It assures that, if nothing can be perfectly accomplished for and by us here and now, then nothing can be definitively lost or missed, and nothing is totally irreparable. . . . The word unfinished suggests infinite. It is a call to a road never closed and barren, a road wide open to life, to everlasting life."[2]

The fact that neither your story nor mine is finished truly is a blessing. No matter how painful the past, no matter how dire the present circumstances, no matter how bleak the future looks, nothing is beyond the scope of God's redemptive power.

Look up Jeremiah 32:17 and write it in the space below.

Isn't that good news? *Nothing* is too hard for our almighty God! In the Savior's hands, the puzzle of your life has no missing pieces.

Let's focus for a few moments on this second powerful truth:

TRUTH #2: Jesus is still writing your story, and He holds all the pieces.

The trouble is our feelings often tell us a different story, don't they? We can't see a way out of a particular situation, we don't know how a relationship can ever be mended, we can't imagine how a debt will be paid or a sickness healed. These are the times we need to run to our heavenly Father. Jesus is writing your story, and He won't stop until all the pieces are brought together. He is at work, even when we can't see where the path ahead of us leads.

Look up Philippians 1:6. What does God promise in this verse? How do you respond to this truth?

_____

_____

_____

Psalm 18:20 declares, "GOD made my life complete when I placed all the pieces before him" (Message). What pieces do you need to bring to God today? If it's helpful, imagine your life as a jigsaw puzzle and picture what pieces appear to be missing. In prayer, place the pieces before your loving Abba (Jesus's affectionate term for His and our Father).

_____

_____

_____

Laying Down What You Never Had

Facing the unfinished quality of our lives and embracing the humility of allowing others into our pain can be quite challenging. You've been going there with me, and I am grateful the Holy Spirit has been our guide. Today I want to look at this one final truth as we close this first session:

TRUTH #3: No matter how things appear, God is in control.

On a scale of 1 to 10, how intent have you been at controlling the circumstances of your life?

1 ←————————————————————→ 10
SURRENDERED   SUPER CONTROLLING

To those of you looking for an 11 on this scale . . . I can relate!

In all honesty, when life feels out of control, my first reaction isn't always to thank God that He is sovereign. Instead, I instinctively want to force life back into control. Perhaps, from personal experience, you know how well that goes!

Life overflows with anxiety-producing, out-of-control circumstances. I don't think it's a coincidence that God tells us not to be afraid well over three hundred times from Genesis to Revelation. By numeric count, the Bible tells us even more often, however, that our God is perfectly sovereign.

Look up the word *sovereign* or the phrase *sovereignty of God* in a Bible dictionary and write the definition below. If you need help accessing Bible tools, try this link: https://www.studylight.org/dictionaries.

_____

_____

God is in all and over all; nothing is outside His control. Indeed, as 1 Timothy 6:15 proclaims, Jesus "is the blessed and only Sovereign, the King of kings and Lord of lords" (ESV). This means not only that Jesus rules over all but also that He is *good* at controlling everything.

I don't know about you, but when I try to control things, the word *blessed* does not come to mind. No one wants to be around a control freak. No one enjoys *being* a control freak either. People may believe they "have to" control things to feel safe, but trying to control everything is actually a miserable way to live. If you operate under the falsehood that everything is up to you, you live with constant disappointment, constant striving, constant tension.

Open your Bible and read Philippians 3:21. How does this verse describe God's power?

_____

_____

Paul reminds us that God can bring *everything* under His control. Do you have the power to bring everything under your control? Take a moment to consider how much of life you can actually control. Write what comes to your mind below.

_____

_____

_____

I spoke frankly with you in chapter 1 of *Holding On When You Want to Let Go*, and I'll remind you here: human control is an illusion. We never could and never will be able to control our lives. We can, however, surrender the control we never had to the God who has had it all along.

If you have ever struggled with control, write a prayer of confession here.

_____

_____

_____

Now write a prayer of praise and thanksgiving to our sovereign God, who promises to control all things and to do it well.

_____

_____

_____

Ask God to meet you in any areas of your life that currently feel out of control. Be honest! Your good Father wants to hear your heart and help you in every time of need. May the words of Hebrews 4:16 help you form a prayer: "Let us come boldly to the throne of our gracious God. There we will receive his mercy, and we will find grace to help us when we need it most."

_____

_____

_____

Finally, rewrite the three main truths we studied in this session, asking the Holy Spirit to seal them in your heart and mind.

1. _____

2. _____

3. _____

Let's live in these truths today!

Holding On When You Feel Alone and God Is Silent

I believe that no matter what we are facing, God's Word speaks to it. So what does it have to say to us when life falls apart and we feel so alone? Even though I see brokenness in myself and in others, even though there are circumstances in life that don't make sense, I know this: God is good, God is love, God is in control. God's Word is alive and can help us make it all the way home.

Sheila Walsh

And the Holy Spirit helps us in our weakness. For example, we don't know what God wants us to pray for. But the Holy Spirit prays for us with groanings that cannot be expressed in words. And the Father who knows all hearts knows what the Spirit is saying, for the Spirit pleads for us believers in harmony with God's own will.

Romans 8:26–27

IN ALMOST EVERYONE'S life, there comes a point when the phrase "hanging on by a thread" becomes all too real. Your child rejects Christ. The cancer comes back. A spouse walks out. When life hurts, the temptation to let go increases.

This is too hard, we may think.

I don't know how we'll get through this.

Where are you, Lord?

I know what pain feels like. I understand.

I remember the deep confusion and loneliness that followed my father's death. A brain aneurism that drastically altered my dad's once loving and kind personality eventually led to his hospitalization and death by suicide. My family never spoke about it. Scottish children didn't attend funerals back then, so I only recall my mother coming home in a simple black dress and hat. Questions and fears nearly suffocated me.

Later in life, before my clinical depression diagnosis, I felt like I was disappearing a little more every day. Nothing I did, no prayer I prayed, no amount of fasting seemed to shake the crushing weight of sadness I lived with. I loved God yet felt miserable. The heavens seemed silent, but God was still working.

But God . . .

When these two words come together, deep truths await us.

Life hurts, *but God* hurts with us.

Anxiety looms large, *but God* is greater than our fears.

Hope seems futile, *but God* never stops working.

In the moments of our greatest pain, when the battle for our hope and joy is raging, the presence of our Lord can become more real to us than ever before. When you feel alone and God is silent, remember these truths:

1. Shame is a liar, but you can anchor yourself to God's Word of Truth.

2. You can worship in the midst of what you don't understand.

3. Even when you can't see God's plan, when you're asked to wait, God is working.

Let's study each of these truths and hold on together to the God who never lets us go.

An Unbreakable Lifeline

The writer of Hebrews knew God intimately. In profound ways, this book of the Bible reveals our heavenly Father, our Savior Jesus, and the Spirit who indwells us. Take a moment to read the following passage.

> When God wanted to guarantee his promises, he gave his word, a rock-solid guarantee—God *can't* break his word. And because his word cannot change, the promise is likewise unchangeable.
>
> We who have run for our very lives to God have every reason to grab the promised hope with both hands and never let go. It's an unbreakable spiritual lifeline, reaching past all appearances right to the very presence of God where Jesus, running on ahead of us, has taken up his permanent post as high priest for us. (Heb. 6:17–20 Message)

In Christ, we have an unshakable and certain hope, a hope that anchors our souls to God Himself. When we fasten our hearts to the Word of Truth, we, too, become unshakable. Not because we've got life figured out but because God's promises never change. God will not—indeed, God *cannot*—break His Word. We know this to be true because Jesus *is* "the way, the truth, and the life" (John 14:6).

Is it easy or difficult for you to believe that God's promises are unbreakable? Why? How does the passage you read from Hebrews 6 intersect with your life experiences?

_____

_____

_____

In the English Standard Version, Hebrews 6:19 describes our hope in God's Word as a "sure and steadfast anchor of the soul." Doing a bit of research on this passage led me to *Thayer's Greek Lexicon*, which points out that anchors haven't changed much since ancient times.[1] They are still used to hold a ship in place. I found that fascinating and, considering we're talking about an inanimate hunk of metal, oddly comforting. Far more comforting is the truth, found later in the book of Hebrews, that "Jesus Christ is the same yesterday, today, and forever" (13:8). Anchors may not have changed much, but our Lord hasn't changed *at all*. He will always be your anchor in a storm.

I don't know about you, but I'm far from unchangeable. Especially when I factor emotions into the equation. My feelings ebb and flow with life's circumstances. That's why I need to anchor myself to God's Word of Truth. Whenever I'm struggling, I open my Bible. That may seem obvious, but for me, God's truth is life and breath. I may not find easy answers, but I find myself in the pages of God's Word. In all my times of self-doubt, of insecurity, I anchor my emotions to the Word of God, and I remember that I'm not alone.

What has your experience with God's Word been like?

_____

_____

_____

Look up John 17:17 and write the words of Jesus in the space below.

_____

_____

Just before His death, Jesus prayed that God would make us holy by His truth. In the same breath, He assured us that His Word is that very truth. If we're not anchoring ourselves to God's truth, we can quickly become untethered by emotions.

Take a moment to confess to God any ways you have undervalued or neglected His Word.

_____

_____

First John 1:9 promises that when we confess our sins, God is faithful to forgive. Whatever your journey with His Word has been like up to this point, you can choose today to anchor yourself—mind, soul, and spirit—to the hope of the world, Jesus, Truth incarnate.

Because of Christ's death and resurrection, we can have unshakable, unbreakable intimacy with God. We are never alone. Why, then, don't we experience this? I've found, in speaking with women around the world, that the enemy uses a particularly evil strategy to separate us from the anchor of our souls. This weapon of mass destruction? Shame.

While we use one word for "shame," the Greek New Testament uses several unique terms. Looking at the original texts allows us to better understand what shame is and how it operates in our minds and hearts. The Greek noun *aischuné* refers to the disgrace or confusion of one who feels exposed. Shame makes you feel as if you've been uncovered. The verb *kataischuno* takes this idea even further, signifying a dishonor that puts to "utter confusion" a person "whom some hope has deceived."[2]

Deceived . . . exposed . . . utterly confused. Perhaps you can see why the enemy favors this strategy?

TRUTH #1: Shame is a liar, but you can anchor yourself to God's Word of Truth.

Theologian Lewis Smedes defined shame as a "feeling that we do not measure up and maybe never will measure up to the sorts of persons we are meant to be. The feeling, when we are conscious of it, gives us a vague disgust with ourselves, which in turn feels like a hunk of lead on our hearts."[3]

Through shame, the enemy attacks the very core of our identity, crushing us under the weight of the secrecy and fear shame breeds. Insidiously, shame focuses not on a bad thing we've done or said but on who we are. "You'll never be good enough. You're defective. Worthless. Inadequate. You don't belong, and you never will," the accuser hisses. As these lies take root within us, shame moves from a feeling to a state of being.

What is your experience with shame? Have you ever felt "less than" or struggled with "not good enough" thoughts?

_____

_____

_____

Shame is a liar, and we must combat it with the truth. I'm so grateful that in the pages of His Word, God reveals His solution for shame: grace. The grace of God triumphs over shame. His grace settles the questions of our acceptance, our worthiness, our value. Because of grace, we are accepted at the depth of our being; we are accepted without the possibility of rejection; we are deemed not merely "good enough" but treasured.

Read Isaiah 43:1–4 and write down the ways God describes you.

_____

_____

God chose you. His grace calls you. In Him, you are precious, honored, and beloved. Breathtaking, isn't it?

Spend some time thanking God for these truths. Confess any ways in which your heart resists what He says about you. Ask God to help you accept His grace on a deeper level, healing you from any shaming messages you may have heard.

_____

_____

Shame will try to make you feel alone and weak. God's truth enables you to hold on when emotions scream at you, "Give up! Let go!" Grace speaks a more powerful word of hope to your heart.

Read 2 Corinthians 12:9. Through the apostle Paul, what does God tell us about His grace?

_____

_____

His grace is what you need, and His grace is enough. When you feel the silent, gnawing ache of loneliness, when the accuser hurls shaming lies at your heart, you can run to God's Word and anchor yourself to His truth. The choice is yours. We can control very little in life, but we can control our choices. You can choose to hang on to Jesus when circumstances tempt you to let go in despair. Will you choose grace with me, letting God's Word triumph over shame and loneliness?

Even If . . .

Grace enables us to overcome shame. Grace redeems our pain, turning the ashes of our heartbreak into something God can use for His glory. Grace does not, however, erase the pain of living in a broken, fallen world. We still experience grief and loss; we mourn; we cry. God not only understands this but also gives us examples—in the Psalms, in Job, in Lamentations—of how suffering transforms us. His Word teaches us the following profound truth as well:

TRUTH #2: You can worship in the midst of what you don't understand.

When you have walked through the valley of the shadow of death and *still choose to love God*, all of heaven celebrates. When you fall to your knees, with questions on your lips and tears on your cheeks, and *still worship God*, all of heaven celebrates.

Read 1 Peter 1:3–12. What does God tell us about suffering, faith, and the watching hosts of heaven?

_____

_____

In *Holding On When You Want to Let Go*, we looked at the story of Job. Even after losing his wealth, his health, and his ten children, Job worshiped God. In the depth of his agony, Job acknowledged God's sovereignty. Despite unfathomable suffering, though his wife encouraged Job to "curse God and die" (Job 2:9 ESV), this remarkable man held on to his Redeemer.

In faith, Job proclaimed, "I know that my *redeemer* lives, and that in the end he will stand on the earth" (19:25 NIV, emphasis added). You'll note that Job didn't say, "I know that my *God* lives, and that in the end he will stand on the earth." With eyes of faith and divine revelation, Job looked through the centuries and saw that Jesus was on His way.

Read Job 1:21 and 19:25–27. In these passages, how does Job worship and show his faith in God?

_____

_____

Take a moment to thank God for the example of this brave man of integrity. If it is difficult for you to imagine facing the kind of suffering Job did and worshiping God in the midst of it, confess that to God. He understands the struggles we face; He does not condemn you. Ask the Holy Spirit to reveal to you that even in your pain, you can see God's goodness with your own eyes (Job 19:27).

_____

_____

_____

God's Word provides another remarkable example of faithful worship in the midst of affliction. Turn to the book of Daniel and read chapter 3. How do Shadrach, Meshach, and Abednego respond to King Nebuchadnezzar's threats in verse 18?

_____

_____

In Daniel 3:24–25, what surprises King Nebuchadnezzar?

_____

_____

Biblical scholars call this a *Christophany*, a moment in history when Christ appeared in human form before His virgin birth. Jesus literally stood in the fire with Shadrach, Meshach, and Abednego, three brave souls who refused to worship any but the living God.

Record King Nebuchadnezzar's response to these dramatic events in Daniel 3:28.

_____

_____

The "even if" faith of Shadrach, Meshach, and Abednego astounded the ancient king who ordered their execution. It astonishes me today. I want that kind of unshakable, "even if" faith. What about you?

Talk to God about this. Tell Him where your faith is today and where you'd like Him to take you. Ask Him to help you worship "even if."

_____

_____

Our Never-Stopping, Never-Failing, Never-Giving-Up God

If you have ever experienced the silence of heaven, I empathize on a deep level. I know how desperate the silence of God can feel. Job endured long days of suffering, waiting for a word from the Lord. During that time, so-called friends heaped shaming messages on Job. "You must have done something wrong; clearly God isn't pleased with you. You better pull yourself together." Job sought answers for the questions "Why?" and "How long?" He desperately wanted to understand. I certainly would have too!

Through Job's experience, however, we see that there are no answers big enough for human suffering. Instead of answers, God gave Job something far better. The Lord gave him—and gives us—Himself. His presence is the good we seek, the balm we need. In Him is the peace, patience, joy, and hope that enable us to hold on when despair tempts us to let go.

Read Psalm 73:28. What does this verse tell us about God's presence?

_____

_____

The nearness of God is the good we long for.

TRUTH #3: Even when you can't see God's plan, when you're asked to wait, God is working.

When agonizing days drag into heartbreaking weeks . . . months . . . even years, we may feel like the door of heaven has been shut and double bolted against us. We believe that God is loving and merciful. We believe that He is a God of all comfort. We believe that He cares for us. We believe that He speaks to His people. We believe and yet we are living with the silence of God. This is when the presence of God can become dearer to us than life itself.

I opened this session with two verses from Romans 8. Please open your Bible and revisit verses 26–27 with me now.

What does this passage tell us that the Holy Spirit is doing when life hurts and words fail us?

_____

_____

Now read Hebrews 7:25. What does this verse tell us about Jesus?

_____

_____

Never forget that Jesus is always praying for you. Never forget that when you can't even utter a word, the Holy Spirit intercedes for you. The silence of heaven does not mean God has stopped working. He has not withdrawn His presence. His nearness is the good you long for, even when you are asked to wait.

Read Psalm 27:13–14. What encouragement can these verses give you when you're asked to wait?

_____

_____

_____

Only the presence of God enables us to hold on when life's pain shouts, "Let go!" Only our never-stopping, never-failing, never-giving-up God is strong enough to anchor us to hope. Christ, the perfect Lamb of God, the One who spoke the world into being, is with you and me . . . right now. Even when we can't see His plan, He is working. Even in the waiting and silence, He is working.

As we close this session, talk to God about waiting, trusting, and the gift of His presence. Confess any struggles. Receive His mercy and ask for the help you need.

_____

_____

_____

Finally, rewrite the three main truths we studied in this session, asking the Holy Spirit to seal them in your heart and mind.

1. _____

2. _____

3. _____

I'm holding on to Jesus. And I'm praying that you will too.

Holding On When You're Afraid

I don't know what's going on in your life right now as you read this, but I want to remind you, my friend, that God keeps His promises. There are situations when we feel betrayed and wounded, and the great temptation is to try to fix things ourselves. We get to choose. We can trust our own ability to untangle a mess, to fight our own battles, or we can hide ourselves in the shadow of the Almighty. We can take our fear to our Father.

Sheila Walsh

Don't be afraid, for I am with you.
Don't be discouraged, for I am your God.
I will strengthen you and help you.
I will hold you up with my victorious right hand.

Isaiah 41:10

I WAS ABOUT TWENTY YEARS OLD, and my brother, Stephen, and I had decided to spend the day in Glasgow. We wandered up and down the busy streets, chatting and window shopping, enjoying the hustle and bustle of the big city, quite a change from the small, seaside town where we grew up.

A stranger approached Stephen and handed him a pen. It was a basic con, the kind in which an unsuspecting victim takes what's offered to him and then "owes" money to the other person. This had happened to Stephen before, and he decided enough was enough. Holding on to the pen, my brother kept walking, ignoring the con man's shouts.

As the stranger pursued us and raised his voice, I snapped. Fear exploded inside me. I began to cry, begging Stephen to give the pen back. Seeing my obvious distress, he did so immediately. Of course, my brother wanted to know what was wrong, but I couldn't explain it to him. It was a visceral fear response, completely out of step with the circumstances. I didn't understand it at the time, but that day I responded to core fears I had never named.

Anger is dangerous.

People can't be trusted.

I have to do whatever it takes to survive.

Years later, God began teaching me that if I don't understand why I react in a particular way, I'll do it again and again. As humans, we long for closure and understanding; we yearn to right the wrongs of the past. We ache to change the ending of stories that have scarred us. Many of our experiences leave us with deep and unspoken fears, fears that control us if we don't confront them *with Jesus*, allowing Him to have the victory and redeem even our most painful stories.

In this session, I'd like to look at three core fears women face. We'll address the lies associated with those fears and then allow the truths we learned in chapter 4 of *Holding On When You Want to Let Go* to conquer the deceptions of fear. My prayer is that in taking our fears to our victorious Savior, we can genuinely change the way we respond to life stressors. If you're ready for that, let's dive in, taking our fears straight to our loving heavenly Father.

FEARFUL LIE	VICTORIOUS TRUTH
This is my fault; I'm getting what I deserve.	Because of Jesus, we get what we don't deserve—and that's grace.
God has abandoned me; He won't follow through.	God always keeps His Word.
If the answer to my prayer is no, I won't be able to make it.	Whether you get the answer you pray for or the answer you fear, God is always with you.

The Difference-Maker

The greatest minds had gathered to discuss comparative religions. Experts debated which, if any, belief set Christianity apart from other worldviews. Systematically, they began to eliminate possibilities. Incarnation? No, other religions include mythologies of gods appearing as humans. Resurrection? No, tales of a return from the dead can be found in cultures around the world. On the debate went . . . until C. S. Lewis entered the room.

"What's all the rumpus about?" he asked. (Yes, he allegedly used the word *rumpus*.)

Lewis's colleagues explained that they had been discussing Christianity's uniqueness, whether any article of faith set belief in Jesus apart from every other religion.

"Oh, that's easy," Lewis responded. "It's grace."[1]

Grace—the unmerited favor of God. The unconditional love given to the undeserving. The beyond-rational, better-than-we-could-hope-for-or-imagine righting of wrongs that we have done. This is the outrageous truth that goes against every instinct of human nature and saves our lives.

You may have heard that grace sets you free from sin. I want you to know that grace also sets you free from fear, especially the fear caused by the lies that so many women believe: this is your fault; this is what you deserve. As Bono, the lead singer of U2, so beautifully articulated, "Grace defies reason and logic. Love interrupts . . . the consequences of your actions."[2] Grace proclaims triumphantly:

TRUTH #1: Because of Jesus, we get what we don't deserve—and that's grace.

Read Psalm 103:8–14. What does this passage teach us about "deserving"? What does it teach about God's amazing grace?

_____

_____

Have you ever been tempted to believe "This is what I deserve. This situation is happening because I did _____ or didn't do _____"? If so, bring these thoughts to your heavenly Father. Confess the ways in which these lies have hurt you. If you have not faced these lies, take a moment to pray about the impact of these lies in others' lives.

_____

_____

_____

As the waves of our past mistakes and wrong choices wash up on the shores of our souls, fear may grip us. When this happens, you and I have a choice. We can run to our gracious Father, or we can run deeper into the darkness of fear. We choose our own adventure, a perilous one or a peaceful one. We get to determine the course our minds will take.

Please allow me to acknowledge that we may not be able to control every *physical* response to fear. When anxieties or worries crop up and regrets over the past loom large in our thoughts, our pulse may race, our breath might shorten. A tightness in our chest or sourness in our stomach might alert us to the possibility of a threat. God wrote these responses into our DNA; they are intended for our good, to help us assess danger and then act. What we do with these signals is what changes our lives. Even when our bodies respond in anxious ways—as mine did the day my brother and I met a con man in Glasgow—we have a choice. The Bible urges us—even more strongly *commands* us—to run to the throne of grace with deliberation and speed.

Read Hebrews 4:14–16. Does Jesus understand our temptation to fear? How does He encourage us to approach our heavenly Father? What can we expect when we go to our gracious God?

_____

_____

_____

When anxious lies plague us, when regret threatens us, we can run—boldly and freely—to our Savior. In His presence, we receive grace and mercy. You may feel the weight of your sin. The scales in your mind may deem your past mistakes heavier than Christ's forgiveness, but that is a lie. Because of Jesus, we get what we don't deserve—and that's grace.

Just before His death, Jesus uttered the words "It is finished" (John 19:30). The original Greek uses the word *tetelestai*, "finished." As I mentioned in chapter 4 of *Holding On When You Want to Let Go*, this word appeared on ancient tax documents. The literal translation? "Bill paid in full." Let that sink in, my friend. Whatever you have done, whatever regrets you might have, whatever wrong paths you may have taken, with His final words Christ stamped on the bill of your life and mine, "Paid in full."

Second Corinthians 5:21 tells us Christ took on Himself what He did not deserve so that we don't have to bear what we do deserve. In the space below, thank God for this truth. Then release to God any mixture of fear and regret you feel. Tell Him that you plan to hold on to His grace and ask for His help.

Taking Back the Territory

Most people—believers and those who claim no faith—can retell the basic story of David and Goliath. The little guy takes down the giant. Very inspirational whether you love God or not. There's so much more to this story, though, and I don't want you to miss some fine—and important—details that help us face our fears and overcome them with truth.

Read 1 Samuel 17:1–11. How does fear factor into this story?

_____

_____

Saul and his men *shook* with fear; terror paralyzed them. Because Saul had not been walking closely with God, the Philistine giant loomed larger in his mind than God's promises. This can happen so easily with our own faith. Lies tell us that we're on our own, that we've got to figure everything out. Fear tells us that God won't follow through on His Word. But the Bible reminds us of this:

TRUTH #2: God always keeps His Word.

As 1 Samuel 17:12–31 records, David arrived on the scene, sent by his father to bring provisions to his older brothers. Remember that David was still a teenager at that point, not old enough to join the Israelite army. He was unceremoniously and unkindly dismissed by his family, but David took none of it. He did not cower like Saul and the rest of the Hebrews. Because David's protector was God, his faith reduced Goliath to size.

Read 1 Samuel 17:32–51. Look especially at verses 45–47. What confidence does David display in this passage? How does this confidence compare to the reactions of Saul and his men?

_____

_____

David made it clear that he trusted in the Lord—and the Lord alone!—to defeat the giant. He entertained no thought of defeating Goliath on his own. That was God's job. True, David got to toss the stone and chop off the heathen's head, but *God won the victory*. A key principle arises from this story: if you want to slay the giants of fear in your own life, you must remember that the battle belongs to the Lord.

Read Zechariah 4:6. In this verse, what does God ask us to surrender, and what does He invite us to receive?

_____

_____

The battle belongs to the Lord. He does invite us to take part in the fight, however. We wage war with the promises of God as our weapons. Trusting in the promises of God, we retake the territory that fear seized.

Turn back to 1 Samuel 17 and reread verse 24. What did the Israelite army do?

_____

_____

Because of their fear, the Israelite army lost territory. The same thing can happen to us. Dear friend, let's determine not to fall prey to this ancient attack of the enemy. Let's retake ground by trusting fully in the promises of God.

Look up the following verses. Write the promise of God and the fear it helps you overcome in the spaces below.

Joshua 1:9 _____

_____

Psalm 100:5 _____

_____

Isaiah 40:31 _____

_____

Nahum 1:7 _____

_____

Philippians 4:6–7 _____

_____

Equipped with God's promises, we can overcome the enemy of fear. We don't do this through willpower but by the power of our almighty God. When the giants of fear loom large, look up. Remember who God is and what He has promised. God's promises changed everything for David, and they can change everything for you and me as well.

God Will Rescue

When you read the five passages outlining God's promises, you may have noticed a consistent theme. God promises to be near us. He will not abandon us nor leave us to our own devices. He promises to be a refuge, a safe place for us to run to. He promises to deliver us, to rescue us.

As we discovered in chapter 4 of *Holding On When You Want to Let Go*, not all rescues look the same. Sometimes we are delivered by God *out of* a situation. He removes the fear or the source of it. Other times, however, we are rescued *in* a set of circumstances. We are empowered to address and conquer fear, even when our situation doesn't change.

The enemy hisses lies like these in our ears:

If God doesn't answer this prayer, you won't make it.

You can't deal with this. It's too much for you.

If God is good, He wouldn't ask you to go through this.

Only one truth can combat these malignant lies.

TRUTH #3: Whether you get the answer you pray for or the answer you fear, God is always with you.

Whether He delivers us out of or in our fears, the rescue of God always comes through His presence. He is the answer we seek.

Have you ever wrestled with unanswered prayers or prayers that were answered in a way that confused you? Perhaps you've watched this happen in the lives of those you love. Take a moment to talk with God about it and write your thoughts here.

_____

_____

_____

Read Psalm 46:1. God made this verse very real to me at 3:00 a.m. the morning after Christian's pediatrician told me he might have leukemia. I begged God to spare my little boy. In what situation do you need God to be your refuge right now? Is it for you? A child? A friend? Ask God to help you in this time of trouble and name those fears.

_____

_____

_____

I received a call the following morning that Christian did *not* have cancer. His condition, anemia, could be easily treated. Barry and I were so grateful, thanking God for this answer to our prayers. Not long after this, while speaking at a conference, I shared this story. At the end, a woman came up to me and told me that she got the other phone call, the one you don't want. She must have seen the look on my face as I thought of how my happy outcome must have been like salt in an open wound to her. She grabbed my hand and said, "No, Sheila, you don't understand. What I'm trying to tell you is this. Whether you get the answer you pray for or the answer you fear, God is with us. He is always with us."[3]

Is this easy or difficult for you to believe? How might it change your life and your experience of fear if you truly believed that God is with you no matter what answer you receive?

_____

_____

_____

For a long while afterward, I thought about my encounter with this woman whose child had to battle cancer. We had both fallen to our knees in prayer; we had both experienced the hand of God reaching down to us. Our outcomes may have been very different, but the one thing we both shared was the gift of God's presence—the gift of His peace—in the midst of our fears.

Read Exodus 33:14–18. What does this passage reveal about God's presence?

_____

_____

Like Moses, we need to determine that we _will not_ move forward without God's presence. God will never leave or abandon us, but that does not mean we won't faithlessly walk away. This is especially common when we don't get the answer we want. We pray, but the job still falls through. We cry out to God, but the illness doesn't go away. We beg, but our children wander farther from their Savior. The answer to these painful situations is never fear. The answer is God Himself.

Read Jeremiah 17:7–8. How does this passage describe the person who trusts in God, even in difficult situations (the year of drought)?

_____

_____

Fear withers you. Trusting that God *is* the answer (as opposed to "gives you an answer") enables you to flourish. When anxious worries tempt you to let go, remember that . . .

God is with you.

He is for you.

No matter what the outcome, His presence will go with you.

Read Zephaniah 3:17. Use this verse to write a prayer of gratitude to God. Thank Him not merely for what He's done but also for who He is.

_____

_____

_____

Finally, rewrite the three main truths we studied in this session, asking the Holy Spirit to seal them in your heart and mind.

1. _____

2. _____

3. _____

Our God is mighty to save! Whether He rescues us *out of* or *in* a situation, He is near. I'm pressing into God's presence today, and I invite you to join me. In His presence is fullness of joy (Ps. 16:11). May nothing hold us back.

Holding On When You've Messed Up

Repentance is not an emotion; it's an action. We can say we're sorry a million times, but if we don't turn around, if we don't change our minds, then nothing changes.

Sheila Walsh

Generous in love—God, give grace!
　　Huge in mercy—wipe out my bad record.
Scrub away my guilt,
　　soak out my sins in your laundry.

Psalm 51:1-2 Message

IT HAD BEEN A RELATIVELY NORMAL 2015 DAY. Our son, Christian, would graduate soon, and—like many empty-nest couples—Barry and I had decided to downsize. After meeting with a realtor who evaluated what we could do to get the best price for our home, we booked a carpet cleaner to "freshen" the upstairs rugs. Or so I thought.

The doorbell rang that fateful day, and the professional man who entered seemed friendly and competent. Excellent. I led him upstairs . . . not knowing it was to my doom.

This kind gentleman—let's call him Rodney the rug guy—suggested a quick scan for any pet stains. Trying not to be offended, I assured him that our dogs were perfect little ladies and entirely house-trained.

I will never forget Rodney's look of pity and authority in equal measure. "How 'bout we just see what turns up," he offered with a smile.

Before I knew it, Rodney plunged his arms into a large carrying case and emerged with what honestly looked like a rocket launcher.

"Ma'am, this is a UV Black Light Urine Detector," he announced, promising me that—although it was safe—what it revealed likely wouldn't be pretty. "Stand back and kill the lights," he ordered.

Nothing could have prepared me for the shock. Words fail me. My bedroom carpet lit up like a pinball machine, flashing a single neon message: "You've been living in a mess, Sheila."

Rodney, observing my aghast silence, put a hand on my shoulder and said, "That's why I'm here, ma'am. I'm a professional. I've been trained to handle this."

Until Rodney illuminated our room with his superhero UV gun, I lived in blissful ignorance. Light revealed what was hidden . . . insidiously hidden.

Light has a way of doing that, doesn't it? Revealing, illuminating, exposing.

And while there's some horror when looking back at my carpet-cleaning fiasco, when Christ shines His light on our lives, revealing, illuminating, and exposing sin, Jesus asks us to respond with repentance, not with justification or offense.

In this session, we'll focus on the following key principles that enable us to hold on even when we've messed up:

1. We've all messed up; that's why Jesus came.
2. To repent means to change your mind, to turn around.
3. There is life-changing power in the name of the Lord.

None More Than Others

Modern culture doesn't favor the word *sin*. It's seen as an antiquated, if not completely irrelevant, idea. "We're all human," the world may acknowledge, "but why do religious people have to label everything as 'bad'?" It's easier to admit "I'm not a perfect person." But to call ourselves sinners? That apparently goes too far.

Not so for followers of Christ. Because of Jesus's death and resurrection, we're called to take sin . . . *our sin* . . . seriously.

Read Romans 3:23 and 6:23. Write down the clear truths about sin that God reveals.

_____

_____

The New Testament noun for "sin," *hamartia*, and the verb for "to sin/ have sinned," *hamatanó*, are related terms, used by archers who miss their target.[1] Sin doesn't just miss a mark, however. Sin misses *the* mark, the whole point of life: to glorify and honor God. In this way, sin is never merely about what we do; it's also about *what we believe* and *who we are*. When we miss the mark by gossiping about friends or cheating on our taxes or repeatedly spending more than we earn, we show God that His standard is less important to us than what we want. This is sin, and—without Jesus—sin leads to death.

Is it easy or difficult for you to identify yourself as a sinner in need of grace? If you are a follower of Christ, you have a new identity as a saint and joint heir with Jesus. While in this mortal body, however, sin will still tempt you to settle for less than God's holiness.

Take some time to ask the Holy Spirit how you might be missing the mark; confess any sin He reveals to you.

_____

_____

_____

Every one of us has missed the mark. No one is excluded. *All* have sinned, according to Romans 3:23. And sin costs us . . . dearly. Paying the price for sin requires death. Jesus came to save us, to pay our debt in full because we've all messed up, not because some of us are more messed up than others.

45

TRUTH #1: We've all messed up; that's why Jesus came.

If you grew up in a community of faith, your church, Christian school, or family and friends will have shaped your understanding of sin. For many churchgoers, sin becomes synonymous with the "big things" those "other people" do—adultery, murder, child molestation. In other words, some of us classify people who sin as fundamentally different from us.

If you had little or no spiritual input growing up, you may have heard that people do good or bad things, but no one is really a bad person at the core. If they just had better education or more opportunities, modern cultural influencers claim, we could all live together in an ideal world. "Imagine" isn't one of John Lennon's most beloved ballads for no reason; people want to think that heaven on earth is possible, if only we all try hard enough. Yet the stark, unwavering message of God's Word is that we are all sinners, every single one of us. Thank God for His eternally-stronger-than-sin gospel.

The gospel is good news because, through Jesus's death and resurrection, we don't have to remain in our sin. In His kindness, wisdom, and grace, Christ purchased our freedom, forgiving our past, present, and future sin.

Read Ephesians 1:6–8. You recently spent some time confessing any way you've been missing the mark by sinning. Now is the time to rejoice and thank Christ for the grace that sets you free. We cannot bring heaven to earth, but we can allow the God of heaven to invade our hearts with grace and truth that set us free.

In *Holding On When You Want to Let Go*, we looked at a particularly grievous time in King David's life. Second Samuel 11 tells us that David made a series of grave mistakes, sinning against God and many others by committing adultery with another man's wife, then arranging her husband's certain death in order to cover up this woman's unplanned pregnancy. This was big. And certainly, in our day-to-day lives, most of the choices we make result in less serious consequences. That said, *every choice* has, at its core, a division of paths. You can walk in the way of light, truth, and righteousness, or you can look to darkness to hide you.

46

Read Psalm 139:11–12 and 1 Corinthians 4:5. What do these passages teach us about light and darkness? What does 1 Corinthians 4:5 teach us about evaluating the sin of others?

I am so grateful for Christ's redeeming love. He's paid my debt—and yours—in full. For some ancient followers of Christ, this led to the idea that they could live however they wanted; after all, Jesus had set them free! Theologians call this heresy antinomianism, literally "against law." This heresy appeals to people who want to believe that because Jesus paid it all, they have nothing more to do. As I'll show you in the next section, this couldn't be farther from the truth.

The Answer

Before I write one more word, I'd like to invite you to join me in a moment of praise and thanksgiving, acknowledging Jesus's eternity-changing sacrifice and unfailing love on the cross.

Write a prayer to thank Jesus for saving you. (Note: If, after reading these first few sessions, you realize that you don't yet have the kind of personal relationship with Jesus that I have been describing, now is the perfect time for you to follow the ABCs. *Admit* you are a sinner and that you need Jesus. *Believe* that He came to earth, died, and rose again to save you. Then *confess* out loud that Jesus is your Lord and Savior. Romans 10:9–10 promises that you will be saved! If you prayed that prayer, tell someone. It's good to confess your new faith to a friend and be encouraged.)

You read Romans 6:23 in the last section. How much does salvation cost?

_____

_____

Salvation is the free gift of God. Hallelujah! We don't have to earn God's favor. His grace is enough for us. What a gift we've been given.

What will we do with this gift? Like those who embraced the antinomian heresy, will we go on sinning without regret? Or will we feel a crushing weight of shame every time we miss the mark after we've confessed Jesus as Lord?

I've discovered that both of these paths ultimately lead to despair. Living how you want eventually crashes down on someone—either you or another person. And, as we identified in session 3, shame is a weight too heavy for any human to carry. Instead, God offers us the perfect way forward. He calls it repentance.

TRUTH #2: To repent means to change your mind, to turn around.

Before Jesus came to earth, his cousin John was born. As John grew, he was filled with the Holy Spirit and lived a set-apart life. A wearing-coarse-camel-hair-and-eating-locusts kind of life. He wasn't auditioning for an ancient survival show, no, he was representing holiness—set apartness—even with his wardrobe and diet. John also preached one consistent message throughout the course of his ministry.

Read Matthew 3:2. What did God command John the Baptist to tell people?

_____

_____

Dictionary.com's definition of *repentance* is "deep sorrow, compunction, or contrition for a past sin, wrongdoing, or the like; regret for any past action."[2] As a child I might have looked at those words and thought, *Yeah, that pretty much settles it.* Over the years the Holy Spirit has helped me see more biblically. Repentance involves but also goes far beyond our feelings or regrets.

Hebrew is a nuanced, rich, and incredibly poetic language. Our English Bibles often miss the captivating beauty of the Hebrew language. For example, *nacham*, one of the Old Testament words associated with repentance, connotes the exhale of a deep sigh of sorrow when faced with the reality of an action. Isn't that powerful and evocative? The word *teshuvah*, also translated "repentance," means "to return" or "a turning back." The stunning beauty of this word lies in the fact that it means an "answer" as well.[3] Your return to Jesus, turning your back on sin and toward holiness, is—literally—the answer.

Read Hosea 14:2. What does this verse teach about confession, repentance, and forgiveness? What part does God do? What are we called to do?

_____

_____

The Greek New Testament gives us additional help in understanding the concept of repentance. *Strong's Exhaustive Concordance*, a resource I highly recommend for those followers of Christ who want to dive deep into God's Word, provides an excellent definition of the Greek word for repentance, *metanoia*. *Strong's* tells us that repentance involves a "change of mind," "after-thought" (as in thinking again about what you've done), even "change in the inner man."[4]

Change in the inner woman. I want that!

At least most of the time I do. Sometimes I cooperate with the work God is doing, and surrender is the biggest aspect of this effort, but other times I struggle and resist God's work. Can you relate?

Do you sometimes participate in and sometimes resist the work of God? If so, take a moment to confess this to the Holy Spirit and ask Him to change you from the inside out.

_____

_____

_____

I shared a story in *Holding On When You Want to Let Go* about how I held back from immediate repentance after I snapped at Barry. He had made some comments to Christian, our son, about dressing more professionally (e.g., not wearing a ball cap) on Zoom video calls, and I responded in a way that can't be called anything but sinful. I could have asked for forgiveness immediately. That would have been the best path, effort fueled entirely by God's grace. Instead, I sat in misery before finally falling on my knees before God. "I repent, Lord," I cried out. "I need you to change my mind. I want to be changed from the inside out, and I'm willing to do whatever it takes."

If you were to evaluate your current thoughts about sin and repentance, how might God want to transform your mind?

_____

_____

_____

In what ways can you surrender more fully to Him, cooperating with His work by following in obedience?

_____

_____

_____

After I repented that evening, God asked me to go to Barry and seek forgiveness. I had been forgiven by God. What a precious and free gift His forgiveness is! I also needed to participate in the "change within me" by humbling myself and asking for forgiveness from my husband. I never feel more whole and holy than when I experience genuine forgiveness. Barry freely and lovingly forgave me, holding no bitterness against me.

Is there someone you're harboring resentment toward? Are you willing to acknowledge that bitterness is a sin that's poisoning you? Talk to God about it and ask Him what your next step of repentance might be (turning around or changing your mind, being changed in your inner person). Then obey whatever He asks you to do, even if it feels scary. I promise, disobedience is far more painful in the long run.

Repentance means changing your mind, turning around. God makes this possible, and He initiates the entire transformation. He also asks us to participate in the process.

When I resist quick repentance, I quickly fall into dark places. Maybe you can relate? We need the light of God to reveal any and every way we've missed the mark. Then, in the repentance He makes possible, we must turn back and allow God to transform us by changing the way we think.

We've got work to do, but we never do it alone. Jesus does all the heavy lifting . . . like a dad who allows his daughter to put a nail in the hefty wooden slat he's already hoisted up the ladder to repair a leaky roof. He allows us to participate by listening to and doing what He says. Through repentance, we get to nail truth into our minds and hearts.

Wonder-Working Power

Repentance brings with it great rewards. We feel the freedom of a clean slate. We sense the joy of our sin-debt canceled. We also get to enjoy greater closeness with the Lord as we walk in His way. Because repentance includes a turning back to Him and a surrender to His work of transformation, we draw nearer to God every time we acknowledge that repentance is the answer. When we call on the name of the Lord for help, He comes quickly to our aid.

TRUTH #3: There is life-changing power in the name of the Lord.

Read Proverbs 18:10. What does this verse teach us about God's name? What does calling on the name of the Lord enable us to do?

_____

_____

God's name holds power—power to save and power to change. When you or I feel like letting go or giving up because we've made mistake after mistake, His precious name draws us back to peace, to joy, to truth.

Look up the following passages and write down the name or names of God revealed in each verse.

Genesis 22:14 _____

Psalm 84:8–12 _____

Isaiah 9:6 _____

John 8:12 _____

John 14:6 _____

Revelation 22:13 _____

You can rest in the power of God's name. He is our Provider, the almighty God, our sun and shield. He is wonderful, the Counselor we desperately need, the Prince of Peace. Because He is light, we don't have to walk in darkness anymore. Because He is the way, the truth, and the life, because He is the first and the last of all eternity, we can trust Him to get us all the way home.

Rewrite the three main truths we studied in this session, asking the Holy Spirit to seal them in your heart and mind.

1. _____

2. _____

3. _____

No matter what you are facing, no matter how hard it is or how dark it feels, there is power in the name above every other name.

Yahweh . . . Jesus . . . Spirit of the living God . . . fall fresh on me and on my sisters and brothers today. May we live in the light and repent quickly when we've missed the mark. We love you, Lord.

Held by the Promises of God

At my lowest point in that year [2020], I made a fresh commitment to dive deep into the Word of God and know for sure what has not and will not change. A steady diet of the evening news and the craziness of social media will give birth to anxiety and fear, but a steady diet of the promises of God will give us an immovable place to stand no matter what else is shaking.

Sheila Walsh

I have told you all this so that you may have peace in me. Here on earth you will have many trials and sorrows. But take heart, because I have overcome the world.

John 16:33

ON THE WHOLE, psychiatric hospitals are not places designed with comfort in mind. Sitting on the cold, tile hospital floor is, admittedly, even less pleasant than lying in a hospital bed, but that didn't matter to me the night I drove—directly from the set of the national television show I co-hosted— three hours to Washington, DC, where I signed myself in for a month of restorative care. Psychiatric care for my diagnosis of severe clinical depression.

After being shown to my room, I was systematically stripped of everything classified as potentially dangerous—even my makeup mirror and blow-dryer.

That morning I had been trusted with a national television audience, but by that evening, I wasn't even trusted with a hair dryer. The nurse was kind, but I felt so alone . . . so afraid. She told me that I would be on suicide watch through the first night. Apparently, I was supposed to rest while being checked on every fifteen minutes. That didn't seem likely, and sleep had eluded me for many weeks, so, taking the blanket from the bed, I sat on the floor, clutching the hospital-issue fabric, huddled in the dark corner.

At some point, I must have drifted off. Or at least I think I did. What roused me was a person entering my room. I assumed that another nurse, performing rounds, had come to make sure I was okay. I didn't even look up.

None of the other nurses had spoken to, let alone touched, me, so I felt rather startled when he laid a hand on my shoulder and placed something small and soft in my hands: a stuffed animal, the kind of gift you might give a child.

A little lamb.

Without a word, he walked toward the door. But before exiting, he turned and looked directly at me. He said only one thing: "Sheila, the Shepherd knows where to find you."

I don't know what prompted you to pick up *Holding On When You Want to Let Go*. From the title alone, you probably knew this was a book and study guide for those who have experienced significant hurt, perhaps even anguish so deep that death seemed preferable to pressing on through the pain.

Beloved child of God, the Shepherd knows where to find you.

In the traumatic memories of your childhood abuse, He knows where to find you.

In the divorce you never wanted and did everything in your power to prevent, He knows where to find you.

In the betrayal of your close friend, in the heartache of an ungrateful child, in the fear of a diagnosis, in the nagging suspicion that none of this will ever make sense . . . He knows where to find you.

The situations are endless, but—praise be to His almighty name—our God is a limitless God. He is a trustworthy Father. A merciful Savior. A tender Shepherd.

The Shepherd knows where to find you, and you are held by the promises of God.

In this session, let's dive into that truth by looking at these three important principles:

1. You did not deserve what happened to you. It was not your fault.
2. God will never fail you or abandon you.
3. God's promises are 100 percent trustworthy—100 percent of the time.

Who Is to Blame?

Humans naturally want to make sense of life. We like explanations, especially explanations we can understand. People are incessant pattern-observers, mystery-solvers, blame-placers. This is not just a modern trait; ancient humans displayed these same tendencies. A notable example is found in John 9, as Jesus ministered in Jerusalem.

> As Jesus was walking along, he saw a man who had been blind from birth. "Rabbi," his disciples asked him, "why was this man born blind? Was it because of his own sins or his parents' sins?" (vv. 1–2)

Who's to blame, Jesus? Whose fault is this? Who sinned, that this man received the sentence of blindness since birth?

I find it interesting that this question came not from the people we might see as the New Testament "bad guys" but from Jesus's own disciples. These are *believers*, people who walked with Jesus and—at least we might assume—would know more about His ways than anyone else. The disciples wanted to know who they could blame.

What about you? Have you ever been tempted to look at a situation and evaluate who is to blame? Have "Well, if he hadn't . . ." or "Maybe if she had . . ." thoughts crossed your mind? Talk to God about this and, where needed, ask for His forgiveness.

Now let's get even more personal. Have you ever wondered if what has happened or is happening to you is your fault? Unburden these thoughts to your Savior. The Shepherd knows where to find you in this pain.

Stop right now and let the voice of Jesus echo in your heart:

TRUTH #1: You did not deserve what happened to you. It was not your fault.

Your Good Shepherd proclaims this over your story, over every piece of your life's puzzle: "You did not deserve what happened to you. It was not your fault." We need to take responsibility for what we have done but *not* for what was done to us.

This is the truth. Our minds and emotions, however, often tell us a different story.

Read John 10:10. According to this verse, who is at work when humans play the blame game?

God's enemy fixates on killing your hope, stealing your joy, and destroying your trust. What does our Lord offer? John 10:10 gives us the answer: abundant life, a rich and satisfying life. Why, then, do we hurt?

Let's look back at the story in John 9 and see how Jesus responded to his disciples' blame-assigning, explanation-seeking questions. "'It was not because of his sins or his parents' sins,' Jesus answered. 'This happened so the power of God could be seen in him'" (v. 3).

How do you respond to this? If you're struggling because your answer doesn't seem "right," it's okay to be entirely honest with your loving heavenly Father. No one is looking over your shoulder, and Romans 8:1 promises that Jesus does not condemn you.

_____

_____

_____

Your reaction may have ranged anywhere from gratitude that God redeems even the most awful stories to outrage that God would allow such pain into someone's life. How can a good God use blindness for His glory when He could have prevented it all along? Okay, so maybe blindness wasn't this man's (or his parents') fault, but why did he have to go through this at all? Isn't there another path to glory, Lord?

I understand these kinds of questions. Over the years, multitudes of people around the world have entrusted their stories to me. Stories of abuse, abandonment, anger, and atrocities I will not even name. Without the tiniest shadow of doubt, I know that God did not "send" these horrible situations into the lives of His beloved children. It is sin's effects that ripple out into all our lives in terrible ways. Because of sin, no one gets through life unscathed. Even Jesus suffered unspeakable pain, culminating in a brutal execution here on earth.

Did He deserve it? Absolutely not!

Was it His fault? In no way.

Christ did not deserve what happened to Him. It was His choice to suffer alongside you. He did this because He loves you. Your Savior wept, He sweat blood, so that you would not have to wonder whether you are to blame.

You did not deserve what happened to you. It was not your fault.

Write 2 Corinthians 5:21 in the space below.

_____

_____

Jesus *became sin*. Don't miss this staggering truth.

The sin that was done to you was laid on Jesus so that you never have to wonder who will carry it. Jesus willingly took every sin so that the blame game could end. He makes you right with the Father so that one day you can enjoy eternal life with no tears, no trauma, no terror.

Read Revelation 21:4. What does God promise about heaven in this verse?

_____

_____

_____

There will be a day, friend, when sighing and sorrow will end, when tears will be wiped away forever, when all doubt and fear will submit to the glory of God's goodness. Until that day, as you walk in the shadowlands here on earth, cling to this promise with me: You did not deserve what happened to you. It was not your fault.

Write a prayer in the space below, asking the Holy Spirit to seal this truth in your mind, heart, and soul.

_____

_____

_____

Never, Not Ever

His arms flailed violently. Breath would not come. Desperation mounted. A child's brain has no context for being drowned by his own father.

Hunter grew up with memories so traumatic that most of us cannot fathom how he survived, let alone surrendered his life to Christ and now serves as a pastor of worship at a large church. His story of redemption brings great glory to God.

Some years ago, however, Hunter could not shake the memory of his psychotically ill father trying to drown him in the bathtub. He was only seven years old, so vulnerable, so much smaller than his muscular dad. Apparently, Hunter's father found his son's attempts to save himself funny, as the memory of his dad's laughter punctuated the nightmares Hunter had about dying underwater, unable to save himself. Desperately needing help to overcome this trauma, Hunter sought care from a trusted Christian counselor.

In working through this experience with his therapist, Hunter encountered Jesus in a life-changing way. During one session, the counselor asked Hunter to revisit that particularly painful event and see where Jesus was while it was happening.

"It was as clear as day," Hunter shared, "and completely unexpected." He drew a deep, almost shuddering breath.

"I saw Jesus tenderly and swiftly pry my father's hands from my head. I emerged from the water, and Jesus wrapped His arms around me, shielding me from further attack. Jesus wept while He held me."

Friend, our stories may not mirror the intensity of Hunter's. I know he is grateful that not everyone experiences the abuse he endured as a child. I am so thankful that many people enjoy happy childhoods, joyful memories, stable health and finances. Still, no one gets through this life without scars.

In the moments of our deepest suffering, we need to cling, without wavering, to this truth:

TRUTH #2: God will never fail you or abandon you.

In chapter 6 of *Holding On When You Want to Let Go*, I shared some information about Hebrews 13:5 with you.

Look up Hebrews 13:5 and write it in the space below. I'll start it for you. "For God has said,

_____

_____

Perhaps you recall that this verse uses a specific grammatical construction, a double negative that renders it, in literal translation, something along the lines of "Never, not ever will I leave you or forsake you." I love that truth! *Never, not ever!*

Now I'd like to turn your attention to a verb in that sentence; the word in your Bible may be *abandon* or *forsake*. Hebrews 13:5 is the only biblical instance of this particular Greek word, *egkataleipó*. The root word for "to leave or forsake" is included elsewhere, but what makes the use of this word in Hebrews 13:5 quite special is the tiniest of details.

Whether you like grammar or not, there is glory in the Lord's use of grammatical constructions. This Greek verb, which uses the aorist tense, subjunctive mood, and active voice[1] (hang in with me here!), indicates that no matter what hypothetical situation you could come up with, it would be impossible for God to break this vow. According to Greek scholars Wilfred E. Major and Michael Laughy, this kind of verb "NEVER has an augment"[2] (all caps theirs, not mine). What that means is that you can't add to it because there would be nothing greater. This is as good as it gets!

How do you respond to this? If it is difficult for you to believe this, ask God to seal the truth in your mind and heart that no matter what happens, He cannot and will not forsake you.

What if it's autism?
What if he's cheating?
What if you lose everything?
What if she relapses?

No "what if" circumstance can overcome God's promise—He will never abandon you. Against this there is no argument.

Take a moment to write a prayer of praise and gratitude to the God who will never leave you or forsake you.

_____

_____

_____

Zero Percent Error

Scientists and mathematicians use hypotheses, establish theories, and measure outcomes. They also value discerning how closely their speculations match reality. In order to determine the relationship between what they expected to happen and what actually occurred, they use a formula called percent error. No known experiment has a 0 percent error. In other words, reality never aligns perfectly with human expectation.

The only things in this universe that we can count on to have no margin of error, no mistakes at all, are the promises of God.

TRUTH #3: God's promises are 100 percent trustworthy—100 percent of the time.

Because God is 100 percent trustworthy and we can trust Him 100 percent of the time, there should be no problem with our placing 100 percent of our faith in Him. However, we know that people rarely exhibit this kind of trust.

In your experience, what holds people back from trusting God 100 percent of the time? What holds *you* back from a 100 percent kind of faith?

_____

_____

The enemy used my childhood trauma and my battle with clinical depression to try to introduce "percent error" into my faith. I'm so grateful that God is victorious over even the devil's most convincing lies. God has taught me, over the course of my journey, to cling to what I know *for certain*, the truths that are *sure* and *unshakable*.

In the Hebrew Old Testament, the words *trustworthy* and *faithful* are often translated interchangeably. The root term, *aman*, is translated as "faithful" over twenty times from Genesis to Malachi. This beautiful word is associated with the picture of a loving father supporting a child, a child who knows they will be sustained, cared for, and carried by their parent.[3] As a child, I longed to know the love of a father. Now I rest in the loving arms of the heavenly Father who has been with me every step of the way. He is your Father too.

Isaiah 25:1 proclaims, "O LORD, you are my God; I will exalt you; I will praise your name, for you have done wonderful things, plans formed of old, faithful [*aman*] and sure" (ESV). After reflecting on this verse, write a prayer of praise and thanksgiving for God's faithfulness.

Look up Deuteronomy 33:27. What word picture does Moses include in this verse to illustrate God's faithfulness? What does God promise to do to the enemy who seeks to kill, steal from, and destroy you?

In chapter 6 of *Holding On When You Want to Let Go*, I outline the significance of three of God's 100-percent-sure, 100-percent-of-the-time promises:

- Nothing can separate us from God's love.
- Everything will work out for our good.
- God will give us new strength.

Read John 10:28–29 and Romans 8:35–39. How do these two passages affirm the truth that nothing can separate us from God's love?

_____

_____

People often struggle to believe the truth found in Romans 8:28, that everything will work out for our good, because they assume this means everything will feel good. Read Romans 8:28 and the verse we opened this session with, John 16:33.

Taking these verses together, what is the difference between everything in life going smoothly and God's 100-percent-true, 100-percent-of-the-time promise to work everything *for* our good and His purposes? If this remains a struggle for you, I invite you to dialogue with God about it in the space below.

_____

_____

_____

Read Isaiah 40:28–31. What does God promise He will do? How does Isaiah describe God's power and ability to keep His promises?

_____

_____

_____

Take a moment to reflect on your own faithfulness to God. Are there any areas in which the Holy Spirit might want to move you toward greater faithfulness to your 100-percent-faithful Savior? Confess these areas to

Him now and receive the promise that your heavenly Father will carry and sustain you as you serve Him.

_____

_____

_____

Finally, rewrite the three main truths we studied in this session, asking the Holy Spirit to seal them in your heart and mind.

1. _____

2. _____

3. _____

Whatever your circumstances, you are upheld by the everlasting arms of almighty God. Jesus weeps as He holds us, experiencing the brokenness of this sin-stained world. He goes after the lambs who feel lost and afraid. Dear one, the Shepherd knows where to find you. You are held by the promises of God.

Held by the God Who Rescues

There was no going back to normal. God's rescue plan had a new normal. Being rescued changed me. Not only that, but His rescue included a depth of grace and glory and the pure joy of being held that nothing else could ever have provided. I don't say that lightly. I begged to die, and now I love to live.

Sheila Walsh

We also pray that you will be strengthened with all his glorious power so you will have all the endurance and patience you need. May you be filled with joy, always thanking the Father. He has enabled you to share in the inheritance that belongs to his people, who live in the light. For he has rescued us from the kingdom of darkness and transferred us into the Kingdom of his dear Son, who purchased our freedom and forgave our sins.

Colossians 1:11–14

ALMOST EIGHTY YEARS later, it's still considered one of the most daring and heroic rescues of recorded history.

World War II neared its end, and only 510 American prisoners of war had survived the brutal Bataan Death March and transfer to an internment camp in the Philippines. Inhumane treatment at the hands of their captors, merciless tropical conditions, disease, and punishing forced labor had claimed the lives of thousands. Because intelligence reports identified close to 7,000 enemy troops in the area, attempting to save the POWs amounted to a suicide mission. Army Rangers went anyway.

They refused to give up.

With the aid of brave Philippine guerillas, US soldiers slipped behind enemy lines and marched thirty-five miles to the mobile base from which the rescue mission would be launched. Disheartening news came from the captain of guerilla forces: "Only a few POWs can walk. They must be carried if you are going to take them out."[1]

The Rangers refused to give up.

After organizing water buffalo carts to transfer the prisoners, courageous Philippine litter bearers to carry POWs, and armed forces to hold back any enemy reinforcements, Army Rangers snuck silently into the prison camp. After overwhelming the guards, the Rangers began liberating their incarcerated brothers, many of whom—sick, disoriented, and suspicious—initially refused to come out of the hiding places they had sought in confusion and fear.

The Rangers refused to give up.

Defying all odds, they rescued all 510 prisoners of war. Historians celebrate this daring rescue mission, known as "The Great Raid," as one of the bravest of all time.[2]

Though separated by decades and circumstance, you and I have something in common with the American POWs liberated at the end of World War II. According to the Word of God, we, too, were held captive by an enemy, in bondage to inhumane forces whose orders included massacre and devastation. We, too, desperately needed rescue. And thanks be to God, our Deliverer not only came but also persisted—despite our confusion, disorientation, and even rejection of the invitation to be rescued. Army Rangers knew they might die. In order to rescue us, Jesus knew He *would* die, a cruel and wicked death during which the sins of all humankind would be laid upon His shoulders.

He came anyway.

He refused to give up on even one of His beloved children.

The Great Raid is celebrated, and it should be. How much more should we celebrate our own liberation by Jesus?

When we're in pain, when we're tempted to let go, celebrating our salvation-rescue enables us to hold on. Let's look at three biblical principles that remind us we are held by the God who rescues:

1. When everything around you is shifting, God's Word remains steadfast.
2. God is committed to your rescue; it's a promise.
3. God can be trusted 100 percent of the time, and your life is not out of control.

On Solid Rock

During His earthly rescue mission, Jesus often spoke of the importance of listening to and obeying His Word. His teachings aren't merely inspirational sayings to post on social media or slap on coffee mugs. They are the rock-solid foundation for a life that can withstand storms, a hold-on-when-you-want-to-let-go life.

TRUTH #1: When everything around you is shifting, God's Word remains steadfast.

In Matthew 7:24–27, Jesus illustrates this in a powerful way:

These words I speak to you are not incidental additions to your life, home-owner improvements to your standard of living. They are foundational words, words to build a life on. If you work these words into your life, you are like a smart carpenter who built his house on solid rock. Rain poured down, the river flooded, a tornado hit—but nothing moved that house. It was fixed to the rock.
   But if you just use my words in Bible studies and don't work them into your life, you are like a stupid carpenter who built his house on the sandy beach. When a storm rolled in and the waves came up, it collapsed like a house of cards. (Message)

Jesus described His teaching as "words to build a life on." How much of your current life is built on the foundation of God's Word? Let me give you a starting example. When I'm anxious or afraid, I remember the truth of Philippians 4:6: "Don't worry about anything; instead, pray about everything. Tell God what you need, and thank him for all he has done."

_____

_____

_____

Jesus acknowledged the difference between "knowing about" God's Word and building your life on its truths. He also warned against just "using" His words and not working them into our lives. Ask the Holy Spirit to reveal any ways in which He might be calling you to transfer knowledge about His Word into daily obedience and write what you hear below.

_____

_____

_____

Matthew 7 finishes with these words: "When Jesus concluded his address, the crowd burst into applause. They had never heard teaching like this. It was apparent that he was living everything he was saying—quite a contrast to their religion teachers! This was the best teaching they had ever heard" (vv. 28–29 Message).

Take a moment to celebrate the truth that Jesus lived everything He said. He didn't just teach us to build our lives on the solid rock; He showed us how. Thank Him for rescuing you and for giving you His Word, the guide for how to walk in the eternal freedom He purchased on the cross. What are you most thankful for?

_____

_____

After Jesus's death and resurrection, His Word continued to reverberate through the indwelling of the Holy Spirit and the teaching of Jesus's apostles.

Read James 1:22–24 and write the main points here.

_____

_____

I check the mirror before I leave the house. At the very least, I want to make sure I don't have anything stuck in my teeth! I imagine that you spend some amount of time in front of a mirror getting ready for the day, just like I do. I wonder . . . what would it look like for you and me to allow God's Word to act like a mirror for our souls? Since Jesus rescued us from darkness, as the verse we opened this session with affirms, don't you think we should be willing to look in the mirror of His Word?

Especially when you're tempted to let go, check yourself in the mirror of God's Word. Go back to your foundation. If you see that you've built any area of your life on shifting sand, if the mirror of God's Word reveals something unsightly, repent and be restored. When everything else is unstable and spinning, God's Word remains steadfast.

Write down one or two ways in which you'd like to more deliberately build your life on the solid foundation of God's Word. Ask God to use His Word as a mirror in your life.

_____

_____

_____

God's rescue mission didn't result in only salvation after death; it also enables you to hold on when the storms of life rage here and now. Jesus is the solid Rock on which you can build your life. His steadfast, never-shifting Word shows you how to live, held by the God who rescues.

My Deliverer Is Coming

When you feel stuck in a bleak situation, it's difficult to hold on. Imagine how easy it would have been for the World War II POWs rescued in the Great Raid to give up hope. Though they could not imagine how rescue would come, it did. As followers of Jesus, we have not only hope but also solid evidence to support the belief that our Deliverer comes through—every time. Chapter 7 of *Holding On When You Want to Let Go* affirmed this:

TRUTH #2: God is committed to your rescue; it's a promise.

Psalm 34:17 makes this beautifully plain: "The LORD hears his people when they call to him for help. He rescues them from all their troubles." What a life-changing promise!

How do you respond to the truth that God hears His people and rescues them from all their troubles? Is this easy or difficult for you to believe? Why?

_____

_____

_____

The Hebrew word translated "rescues" in Psalm 34:17 is a rich and nuanced term. The root verb, *natsal*, is used more than two hundred times in the Old Testament, most often to describe God's rescue and deliverance from enemies and evil. It also carries another fascinating meaning: to plunder or to strip.[3]

Read Exodus 12:36. What did the Israelites do to their captors when God delivered them from slavery in Egypt?

The truth we see here is that when God rescues us, He also provides for the journey ahead. He promises not only eternal deliverance but also help out of our trouble here and now. God's rescue strips the power of the enemy, and He uses the spoils of His victory over sin and death to equip you.

This is a truth worth celebrating, and David does just that in Psalm 34:1–3:

> I will praise the LORD at all times.
>> I will constantly speak his praises.
> I will boast only in the LORD;
>> let all who are helpless take heart.
> Come, let us tell of the LORD's greatness;
>> let us exalt his name together. (vv. 1–3)

Write your own prayer of praise and thanks to God for rescuing you.

The New Testament uses three primary verbs for "to rescue"—*sózó*, *rhuomai*, and *exagorazó*. *Sózó*, which appears more than a hundred times in the New Testament, can mean "to preserve one who is in danger of destruction, to save (i.e., rescue)." We see this usage in Matthew 8, when Jesus's disciples encounter serious trouble while crossing the Sea of Galilee.

Read Matthew 8:23–27. *Sózó* appears in verse 25 when—overwhelmed by the fierce storm that struck their boat—the disciples shout, "Lord, save us! We're going to drown." Is there an area of your life that feels so overwhelming that you fear you might drown? Take this opportunity to write a prayer to the God who rescues. If you are not currently facing a storm, pray for someone you know who is afraid and overwhelmed.

_____

_____

_____

In Matthew 8:26, Jesus calmed the storm and addressed the disciples' lack of faith. Spend a moment confessing any areas in which your faith has been too small. Ask the Holy Spirit to fan your faith into flame.

_____

_____

_____

Apart from meaning "saving one from danger or preserving one's physical life," *sózó* is also used to describe salvation from sin. It also carries the connotation of being made whole or complete. When you're tempted to let go and give up, when the pieces of your life feel scattered or even lost, remind yourself that God doesn't just rescue you by the skin of your teeth; He makes the puzzle of your life complete. His rescue makes you whole.[4]

How does it encourage you to know that God's rescue will make you whole and complete?

_____

_____

_____

The other two Greek verbs that can be translated "to rescue," *rhuomai* and *exagorazó*, provide beautiful word pictures illustrating how we are held by the God who rescues. *Rhuomai* carries with it the idea of a Deliverer drawing the rescued one to Himself.[5] It can be a close and intimate way of viewing God's rescue mission. *Exagorazó* means to rescue from loss, as in to "properly, take *full advantage* of, seizing a buying-opportunity, i.e., making the most of the *present opportunity* (recognizing its *future gain*)."[6]

Why is this important?

Because God does not simply rescue you and drop you off somewhere to fend for yourself. He rescues you *and* draws you close to Himself. He delivers you *and* helps you redeem your losses. What an amazing Savior we have!

Read Galatians 4:4–7, which uses the Greek verb *exagorazó*. How does God describe His rescue mission in this passage?

_____

_____

As a beloved daughter of the King, you are drawn near as you are rescued. You are made whole, complete. God can turn the most desperate situations into opportunities to strip the enemy and redeem losses. His rescue gives us a new normal. True, God's rescue sometimes feels like a severe mercy; I spoke openly about that in chapter 7 of *Holding On When You Want to Let Go*. I know it is difficult to hold on. But oftentimes, as the richness of both the Hebrew and the Greek words we looked at illustrates, it is more important to remember that we don't even have to do the holding. Indeed, *we are held* by the God who rescues.

Remind Me Again?

In his masterpiece of practical theology, *Mere Christianity*, C. S. Lewis quoted Dr. Samuel Johnson: "People need to be reminded more often than they need to be instructed." Indeed, Lewis explained, "The real job of every moral teacher is to keep on bringing us back, time after time, to the old simple principles which we are all so anxious not to see."[7]

One of the simple principles that people around the globe find easiest to forget (or are anxious not to see) is that we are *not* in control. By essential contrast, God *is* in control—all the time. Please allow me to remind you again of the final, transformative promise we looked at in chapter 7 of *Holding On When You Want to Let Go*:

TRUTH #3: God can be trusted 100 percent of the time, and your life is not out of control.

We've covered a lot of ground since we first looked at control in session 1. How has studying God's faithfulness, His commitment to rescue, and the solidity of His Word helped you to trust God more completely? If you find you are still struggling with fears about letting go and trusting God's sovereign control, confess them here. There is no condemnation in Christ Jesus (Rom. 8:1), and He is close to the brokenhearted (Ps. 34:18).

_____

_____

_____

Read Isaiah 55:10–13. In this passage, what does God promise He is able to do? How do the word pictures God uses help you to understand His power and love for you?

_____

_____

When life feels out of control, we often seek explanations. This is understandable, but rarely helpful. Let's look at the verses in Isaiah 55 that directly precede the beautiful promises of God's power and love for another important reminder.

Read Isaiah 55:8–9. How do these verses contrast our human limits and God's glorious limitlessness?

_____

_____

I find that passage incredibly liberating. Most of the time, I cannot afford to think my own thoughts, especially when life feels out of control. Instead, I desperately need to know that God's thoughts are higher than mine and that with His eternal perspective, He sees both the beginning and the end. This brings great comfort to me and can to you as well. It means letting go of the control you never had to embrace the God who holds all things.

Read Isaiah 55:3. What does God promise will be yours if you come to Him with listening ears and an attentive heart?

_____

_____

I know how difficult it can be to let go of the control you've tried so hard to keep. I've practiced this kind of surrender for many years now, however, and can assure you that—as you witness God's faithfulness over and over, as you spend more time in His Word than with your fears—trusting God's sovereignty *does* become easier.

Take a moment to write a prayer of praise and thanksgiving for God's promise that He will sovereignly direct your life, even when fierce storms strike. Confess any remaining areas in which you need to trust Him more completely and ask Him to help you hold on to Jesus and let go in faith.

_____

_____

_____

Finally, rewrite the three main truths we studied in this session, asking the Holy Spirit to seal them in your heart and mind.

1. _____

2. _____

3. _____

You are held by the God who rescues. His Word is sure when everything else is shifting. His promised rescue *will* come, and His sovereign power does not fail. We may not see how right now or ever, this side of heaven. But His promises *will not* fail. Rest in that truth today. When despair tempts you to let go, Jesus promises to hold you. He is holding you right now.

Held by the God of Miracles Who Changes Everything

As you think about your life as it is right now with all that's working well and all that's falling apart, do you see yourself as a miracle? I do. But it might mean looking at miracles in a different way. . . .

I'm not fixed. It's much better than that. I'm redeemed, I'm rescued, I'm being held by the One who changed everything. You are too. It really is okay not to be okay. You don't have to be perfect. You are perfectly loved just as you are.

Sheila Walsh

God can do anything, you know—far more than you could ever imagine or guess or request in your wildest dreams! He does it not by pushing us around but by working within us, his Spirit deeply and gently within us.

Ephesians 3:20 Message

WHAT DO YOU think of when you read the word *change*?

For some, this word sparks excitement. *What's around the corner? It could be something wonderful! Let's go and see!*

For others of us, well, change is not nearly as exciting. We tend to assume that change means something *bad*, something that will upend life even further. This attitude may be a temperament issue—the glass is half empty sort of thing—or it may be the result of many difficult years of struggle. For some, change has, more often than not, brought trouble and heartache. Even if people in these circumstances began life with a courageous, hopeful perspective, the school of hard knocks has taught them to view things differently.

I fall into this category.

My early childhood days were filled with tree-climbing, an attempt to fly out of my parents' bedroom window with an umbrella, and fearless energy. After my father's death, as my family faced devastating grief, financial loss, and ongoing struggle, I withdrew from life in so many ways. In most instances, I became fearful and reserved. I constantly felt alone, whether surrounded by friends, colleagues, or concertgoers listening to me sing. *Change* was not my friend. It was something to be afraid of, not excited by.

How do you view change?

I thank God that throughout the decades since life's pain first changed me, I have learned to embrace the God who changes everything. He is the God of miracles, and the greatest miracles happen around and within us every day, if only we have eyes to see.

Let's look at three of the biblical truths we learned in chapters 8 and 9 of *Holding On When You Want to Let Go*. These principles, in the hands of the God who changes everything, enable us to embrace how God is redeeming our lives right here, right now:

1. Miracles change our circumstances; obedience changes our hearts.
2. Jesus knows you, He understands you, and He will never let you go.
3. You don't have to be fixed; you're redeemed.

What Do You Want?

Even those who don't follow Jesus recognize that He was a master communicator. His use of moral teaching, parable, and even irony continues—more than two thousand years later—to impress the most critical minds.

Jesus also used perfectly posed questions to get right to the heart of a matter. One of the questions He used on several occasions strikes me as particularly interesting. The Gospel writers reveal that just before performing a miracle, Jesus would ask a person in dire circumstances some form of the question, "What do you want?"

Read Mark 10:45–52. What happens before and after Jesus asks this question?

_____

_____

Does it strike you as at all odd that Jesus asked a man who was *clearly* in need of a miracle what he wanted? Was there a chance the man might have asked for something other than sight?

_____

_____

Let's contrast this story with John 5, when Jesus asked another suffering man what he wanted. Read John 5:1–7. How did this man respond to Jesus?

_____

_____

In both stories, we find people who desperately needed a miracle, a miracle only God could perform. As you read, however, the blind man, Bartimaeus, and the man who had been sick for thirty-eight years responded very differently to Jesus. Let's look back at John 5 to see what happened after Jesus asked his pointed question.

Read John 5:8–15. What did this man do after Jesus healed him? Did He demonstrate faith in Jesus as a result of his miraculous healing?

_____

_____

In both stories, Jesus performed a stunning miracle. He changed the circumstances of both suffering men dramatically and instantaneously. Only Bartimaeus experienced a change of heart, however. The man who lay crippled and ill for thirty-eight years hastened to the Jewish leaders who would eventually arrest and crucify Jesus, whereas blind Bartimaeus received his sight and changed the entire course of his life. "Instantly the man could see, and he followed Jesus down the road," Mark 10:52 records.

The Bible makes this abundantly clear:

TRUTH #1: Miracles change our circumstances; obedience changes our hearts.

So let me ask you: Do you want a miraculous change of circumstance or a change of heart?

Take a moment to dialogue with God about this. Remember, He already knows what is in your heart. Now is the perfect time to be honest, to confess any ways in which you might have gotten off course.

If you're anything like me, the pendulum of your life probably has swung between wanting God to change you and wanting God to change what's happening to you. I understand desperately wanting a miracle that will transform a situation. I have been there. And there is nothing wrong with crying out to God for healing, just as Bartimaeus did. In fact, when people tried to "shut him down," Mark 10:48 tells us that Bartimaeus cried out all the louder, "Have mercy on me!"

In what area of your life do you need mercy today? Is it for your health? Your marriage? A hurting child or dear friend? I invite you to cry out to the God of mercy right now.

Sometimes when we cry out to God, we receive the miracle we hoped for—the cancer doesn't spread but actually shrinks; your child who had walked away from God returns with fresh passion; the circumstances in our homes or workplaces change—and we cannot contain our gratitude for the miracle God has worked.

Other times our suffering persists. We cannot force an angry, addicted, or abusive family member to change; we watch as a beloved one fades from life because their cancer, ALS, or Parkinson's cannot be cured; mental illness in your family remains a daily struggle.

If, like me, you've been fortunate enough to know one of God's children who believes *even if* they don't receive the miracle for which they pray, you'll know that the greatest miracles of life happen when God's people choose to worship Him right where they are.

Do you remember reading in chapter 8 of *Holding On When You Want to Let Go* the story of my friend John, who found himself in a wheelchair after a life-altering car crash? Fifteen years into his "new normal" as a paraplegic, John and I both served at an event where the visiting evangelist promised healing to all who would believe. John did not get up and walk that night, and I knew it was not the result of his lack of faith. That evening as the evangelist left, I felt angry and sad, but John—looking at the tears in my eyes—responded with miraculous faith.

"Don't be sad, Sheila," he said. "I know God could have healed me, and until He does, I'll worship Him from here."[1]

What about you? Will you worship Him from here? Will you worship Him whether or not your circumstances change?

I am so grateful that God still performs miracles. People receive healing. Marriages are restored. Circumstances do change. I'm also grateful that the miracle of faith is possible for all of us, each and every day. We can be transformed, however much or little our situation changes.

Spend a few moments affirming to God your desire to worship Him right where you are. I realize this will be more difficult for some of you than others. There is no need to rush. As Psalm 56:8 promises, He knows every sorrow and collects every tear. Ask the God of miracles to hold you right where you are.

Fully Known, Fully Loved

Some people seem easier to get to know than others. My beloved husband, Barry, is the consummate extrovert. While he may not be *entirely* an open book, I rarely have to wonder what's on his mind; he tells me! I tend to process things internally. People who listen to me speak or read what I write often tell me that they "feel like they know me," and I am so grateful that God allows me to have this kind of fellowship with sisters and brothers in Christ around the world.

Still, what I speak and write reflects only a fraction of my heart and mind. Whether you are an extrovert like Barry or an introvert like me, you'll know this: there are parts of our lives, our thoughts, our hopes and longings that are never fully known by anyone else.

That's why I am so grateful that this truth is also undeniable:

TRUTH #2: Jesus knows you, He understands you, and He will never let you go.

Read Jeremiah 17:7–10. According to this passage, who knows the human heart? How can the fact that God knows even the sins and temptations with which we struggle encourage us?

Look up the following verses and write down what you learn about the God who knows and understands you.

Psalm 139:1–18 _____

_____

_____

Nahum 1:7 _____

_____

_____

Matthew 10:29–31 _____

_____

_____

John 10:14–15 _____

_____

_____

Don't miss the transformative power of these stunning truths:

- The One who created you has loved you since before your birth.
- The God of miracles knows every single hair on your head.
- The almighty God knows those who take refuge in Him.
- The Good Shepherd knows you and allows you to know Him.

When the storms of life shake you to the very core, remember that God knows you even better than you know yourself!

Read 1 John 3:20. What does this verse teach us about God's greatness? How can that truth help you to hold on when despair tempts you to let go?

_____

_____

God knows you, loves you, and understands you. Period. What a miracle! There is nothing hidden from Him, and that is a tremendous blessing. You can come out of hiding and cast your burdens on the One who cares for you. He will never let you go. Placing your faith in Him day after day makes *you* a miracle. You are held by the God of miracles who changes everything.

Your Redemption Story

Over the last ten years, a plethora of "fixer-upper" television shows have mesmerized literally millions of viewers. Not only are these programs wildly popular, but many of the personalities associated with them have become celebrity-heroes. There's no real mystery why; people *love* renovation stories. They love before and after celebrations. They love watching extreme makeovers of all varieties. And if you ask me, this springs from a truth that God placed deep in the human heart: we all want to be redeemed.

I've been asked more times than I can count whether God has "fixed" or "cured" my depression. I understand why people want that to be the end of my story. And my God who does miracles could certainly change my neurological chemistry and "right" my brain. I've discovered, however, that far more miraculous than being "fixed" is being truly and eternally *redeemed*.

For you, too, this principle holds:

TRUTH #3: You don't have to be fixed; you're redeemed.

Redemption means that even if your situation isn't fixed, things can change anyway. Redemption means that although the pain of the past isn't

86

erased, the bitterness no longer needs to flow into your heart. Theologian Lewis Smedes calls this "redemptive remembering." He writes:

> There is a healing way to remember the wrongs of our irreversible past, a way that can bring hope for the future along with our sorrow for the past. Redemptive remembering keeps a clear picture of the past, but it adds a new setting and shifts its focus. . . . Redemptive remembering is focused on love emerging from ashes, light that sheds darkness, hope that survives remembered evil.[2]

We find a powerful example of this in the life of God's servant Joseph, who was trafficked by his brothers into slavery, falsely accused of sexual assault, imprisoned in Egypt for many years, and ultimately brought by God into a place of honor as Pharaoh's second in command.

Read Genesis 50:20. How did God redeem Joseph's circumstances? How is Joseph an example of redemptive remembering?

The primary purpose of the Bible is redemptive. It's God's story of redeeming His people to Himself. He enfolds our redemption story into His own glorious purposes. You are far more than a fixer-upper. You are a priceless treasure whom God paid the highest price—Himself—to redeem.

Read Psalm 130:7. How does God describe His redeeming love?

Read Isaiah 62:1–12. How do the names God gives His people show His commitment to redemptive rescue?

God could certainly fix us up and make us presentable. He does far better than that though. He miraculously redeems our past and transforms our future. I praise God that His miracle of redemption continues each and every day. There is not one moment He is not actively working on our redemption stories, weaving them into His glorious design for the grand redemption story that will culminate with the wedding feast of the Lamb (Rev. 19:6–8).

Read Isaiah 51:11, a prophetic description of heaven. What results from God's eternal redemption?

_____

_____

In chapter 9 of *Holding On When You Want to Let Go*, I took you on a journey with Jesus, looking again at His story and noticing things we might have missed—or never learned.

To remind you:

- Jesus was born among the Levitical shepherds in a birthing cave reserved for sacrificial lambs. He was rubbed with salt, just as the Old Testament offerings required (Exod. 12:5; Lev. 2:13; Luke 2:8–12).
- Jesus fulfilled hundreds of Old Testament prophesies, including those of Isaiah 53, which predicted the cruel manner of His death and the redemption it would provide for us.
- In humility, Jesus bent low to lift us up (Matt. 3:13–17; Phil. 2:5–11).
- To redeem us, Jesus carried our sin on the cross, experiencing separation from His heavenly Father and from his earthly mother (Matt. 27:46; John 19:26–27; Gal. 3:13).
- The grave could not hold Jesus! *Redemption* is a resurrection word (Luke 24:5–6).
- Jesus redeemed Peter, the disciple who denied Him. Instead of disregarding or sidelining Peter, Jesus used him to strengthen his brothers (Luke 22:31–34).

Isn't God's redemption story breathtaking in its scope, depth, and power?

Which of these aspects of Jesus's story helped you to better understand His love and redemptive purposes?

_____

_____

_____

Write a prayer of praise and thanksgiving to your Redeemer. If you've ever been more focused on behavior modification than heart transformation, confess to Him the ways in which you've settled for being a fixer-upper project rather than a redemption story. Ask God to reveal the ways He is weaving your story into His plan for eternal redemption.

_____

_____

_____

Rewrite the three main truths we studied in this session, asking the Holy Spirit to seal them in your heart and mind.

1. _____

2. _____

3. _____

It will be quite something when we've all finally made it home. In heaven, we will understand the entire, amazing redemption story. We will see so clearly that Christ came for one purpose: He came to pay the price for sin. He came to give us a way back home to God our Father. Every single piece of our small redemption stories will be placed in the grand puzzle of God's glorious purposes. We will fall in worship! Why should we live any differently now?

Let Go!
You Are Being Held

I don't know what the missing pieces in your story are. I don't know the circumstances you find yourself in right now or why you might feel as if you are just clinging to hope by a thin thread. But I do know this.

> You are not alone.
> You are not abandoned.
> You are seen.
> You are loved.
> You are believed.
> You are forgiven.
> You are free.
>
> Sheila Walsh

Don't be afraid. Just stand still and watch the LORD rescue you today.

Exodus 14:13

OUR SON IS twenty-four years old, and we could not be prouder of the man he's become. Christian is now a graduate student, on his way to changing the world, but I remember—as if it were only a short time ago—his first day of kindergarten.

The tiny tennis shoes he wore that day have been replaced by footwear so large I honestly wonder if they could double as canoes. He's six feet tall today, but he was my little boy not too long ago. Back then he seemed so young for all-day school, but it was time; I needed to let him go.

Do you remember your first day of school? Or the first day your son or daughter left the house, armed with only a backpack and lunch box, about to face the classroom or homeschool co-op for the very first time?

It was kind of scary, wasn't it?

There were just so many unknowns, but you had to let go.

I suppose I could have clung to what "had been." I could have kept every pair of his tiny shoes (I did keep a few) and every school year's backpack (I did keep one) preserved in acid-free boxes. But that would have been silly. I needed to let some things go.

Because God blessed me with only one child, I wondered not only how Christian's life would change as he went to school but also how my life would change. I needed to let go of what had been and trust God with what lay ahead for both of us.

So much of life is about letting go, isn't it?

Sometimes we're asked to let go of things we know we can't hold on to indefinitely. Our children *do* grow. People move away and relationships *do* change. We *do* age (even Olay won't argue that; they just want you to "defy" aging, whatever that means).

And then there are the times we dread, the times we're asked to let go of something we hoped would last forever.

I know how painful letting go can be.

No matter what kind of letting go we are asked to face, as followers of Christ, we can move forward with confidence, remembering that when we let go in faith, we are held in the arms of our all-loving, all-powerful, all-knowing Savior.

Dear friend, you can let go today. And you can do it because Jesus's arms are strong enough. In this final session, let's look at the following three truths that enable us to let go, not in despair but in faith, utterly convinced that because of Jesus, we are being held:

1. In difficult places and apparently hopeless situations, we can say, "This looks impossible, *but God.*"
2. The missing pieces of your story are in the safest hands of all—Jesus's.
3. The best is yet to be; it's a promise.

Impossible Things Are Happening Every Day

Have you ever heard the saying "When life hands you a lemon, make lemonade"?

The man who wrote that line, Norman Vincent Peale, helped found—whether intentionally or not—the modern self-help movement. His 1952 book, *The Power of Positive Thinking*, stayed on the *New York Times* bestseller list for 186 consecutive weeks. That's almost three straight years of people buying, over and over and over again, Peale's guide for how to reverse negative circumstances with a positive mental attitude. Peale wrote, "So to overcome your obstacles and live the 'I don't believe in defeat philosophy,' cultivate a positive-idea pattern deeply in your consciousness. What we do with obstacles is directly determined by our mental attitude. Most of our obstacles, as a matter of fact, are mental in character."[1]

I've no doubt that Mr. Peale had some wonderful things to say. But the idea that *most* of our obstacles can be overcome with the power of positive thinking might feel like a slap in the face to many in the world.

Can positive thinking eradicate poverty and homelessness?

Will a positive mental attitude end racism and oppression?

Will Peale's prescribed "positive-idea pattern" topple cruel leaders, establish world peace, cure every terminal illness, and set captives free?

For even the most positive of thinkers, this is impossible.

I thank God that the world's future does not rest on my or your ability simply to "be positive." Neither you nor I will ever let go and trust God if it all comes down to us—to our abilities or our positive thinking.

We can let go with confidence *only* when we know we are held by a God who specializes in the impossible. When you feel tempted to give up, don't try to simply "think positive." Instead, lean into what we learned in chapter 10 of *Holding On When You Want to Let Go*:

TRUTH #1: In difficult places and apparently hopeless situations, we can say, "This looks impossible, *but God*."

Read Luke 1:37 and write it in the space below.

_____

_____

Such a simple sentence. Such transformative power.

"For the word of God will never fail."

"Nothing will be impossible with God" (ESV).

"For with God nothing [is or ever] shall be impossible" (AMP).

As J. B. Phillips translated Luke 1:37, "No promise of God can fail to be fulfilled" (Phillips).

What God gives us goes so far beyond positive thinking. He gives us access to His never-failing, always-ready, eternally-the-same power and presence. With Him, nothing was, is, or ever will be impossible.

We can let go in faith, held in the arms of our loving Father.

Read Mark 10:23–27. What did Jesus tell His disciples about the power of God and the abilities of humankind?

_____

_____

Jesus gave this explanation to His disciples after being addressed by a rich young man who, unwilling to surrender his many possessions, went away from Jesus *stugnazó*, "sad . . . like a sky covered by clouds."[2] What a striking picture! Refusing to let go leaves us with sorrow that clouds the skies of our minds and hearts.

Take a few moments to allow the Holy Spirit to search your heart. If there is any way in which you've refused to let go, now is a perfect time to entrust yourself to the God who will hold you. Confess any ways you've tried to hold on—to control, to possessions, to anything other than Jesus—and affirm your desire to be held by your impossible-doesn't-live-here God.

94

The same Greek word translated "impossible" in Mark 10:27, *adunatos*, is also used in Hebrews 6:18.

Read Hebrews 6:16–18 and write down what verse 18 calls "impossible."

I just love how the English Standard Version renders this passage: Because "it is impossible for God to lie, we who have fled for refuge might have strong encouragement to hold fast to the hope set before us" (Heb. 6:18).

God will never trick you, manipulate you, or cheat you. He will not lie. He will not fail. I don't know what you're facing today. Your circumstances may feel impossible.

But God so loved you . . . that He sent His son (John 3:16).

But God, being rich in mercy, even when we were dead in our trespasses, made us alive together with Christ (Eph. 2:4–5).

In this world, we will have trouble . . . *but God* has overcome the world (John 16:33).

Which of these "but God" verses encourages you most today? Thank God for this truth and ask Him to help you apply it to your present circumstances.

You have a choice, beloved child of God. You can choose to let go in faith and be held by your God. Will you choose that today?

Your Missing Piece

In 1976, children's author Shel Silverstein wrote a delightful little book called *The Missing Piece*. The story opens with these words:

> It was missing a piece.
> And it was not happy.
> So it set off in search
> of its missing piece.
> And as it rolled
> it sang [a] song.[3]

The "it" in Silverstein's *Missing Piece* story resembles a pizza with a slice taken out of it; it rolls along, singing a song, looking for the missing piece that will complete it. After rejecting several bad fits, it discovers a compatible slice, only to realize it can no longer sing with this piece in place. Silverstein once observed, "'I could have ended the book there' . . . meaning where the piece seemed to have found its mate. 'But instead, it goes off singing: it's still looking for the piece. That's the madness of the book, the disturbing part of it.'"[4]

In a book of fewer than five hundred words, Silverstein identified three things all humans sense, though few understand: (1) every one of us longs for completeness, (2) we look for it everywhere (often obsessively), and (3) no fit on earth, even the most seemingly perfect fit, will allow our hearts to sing as they were created to sing.

Only One, high above the heaven and the earth, can complete us. Only God can make us *both* whole *and* able to sing. Only with Him are the missing pieces of our stories safe. As you read in chapter 10 of *Holding On When You Want to Let Go*:

TRUTH #2: The missing pieces of your story are in the safest hands of all—Jesus's.

Read James 1:2–4. What words does James use in verse 4 to describe those who have been refined by trials and trouble?

_____

_____

Depending on which translation you are currently using, you may have identified words like *complete*, *perfect*, *mature*, or *needing nothing*. The idea here is a puzzle in which every piece has been fitted together.

James 1:4 uses two Greek adjectives that can both be translated as "complete"—*teleios* and *holokléros*.[5] *Holokléros* means "complete in all respects . . . sound . . . entire . . . whole."[6] *Teleios*, on the other hand, is used to convey a completeness that unfolds through necessary stages. There is a *tel-* ("aim") to this process; it leads somewhere. Imagine an old-fashioned telescope that must extend out incrementally to reach its full strength.[7]

Taken together, these words in James 1:4 reveal that when we feel like letting go in despair, when the pieces of our lives feel scattered and we don't know how to hold on one minute longer, God is at work. This is where our faith comes in. We can let go because we know we are being held by our Father. He is completing us. He is in both the perfection *and* the process.

If you're like me, "the process" is often difficult to endure. How might knowing there is an aim and purpose help you approach the unfolding of your completeness with greater patience and peace?

_____

_____

_____

Consider this with me for a moment: God could have "ended" our stories when we accepted Jesus as Savior. In that moment, when we were made eternally complete by the perfect sacrifice of our Lord, we could have been whisked away from earth and into the presence of Christ. Instead, we remain on earth to keep singing, to continually be completed.

It's in the mystery of the already but not yet that we live.

We are already complete in Christ. But we are not yet at home with Him. Until that day, the missing pieces in our stories must come together in His perfect timing, His perfect will.

Read Romans 12:2. What three words does Paul use to describe the will of God?

_____

_____

The Greek word *teleios* makes another appearance here. God's will reaches its "perfect" or "complete" end in us through an unfolding process. God's will never changes, but it always transforms us. And as we pass through each necessary stage of maturity in Christ—a process often called sanctification—we grow stronger, clearer, more purposeful (John 17:17; 1 Thess. 5:23). We cling less and trust more. We let go in faith because we know we're held.

How committed are you to letting God's will unfold in your life? What, if anything, is holding you back from letting go and trusting Him to hold you? Talk to God about it, using the space below.

_____

_____

_____

Second Samuel 22:20–21 reads, "He stood me up on a wide-open field; I stood there saved—surprised to be loved! GOD made my life complete when I placed all the pieces before him" (Message). Write a prayer of praise and thanksgiving to the God who makes your life complete, the God who saves you and loves you.

_____

_____

He is placing each of the pieces of your story in the right place at the right time. We don't always get the big picture; in other words, you and I can't always see the picture on top of the puzzle box. But we can choose to let go and be held by the God who puts things right and makes them complete . . . now and forever.

Good, Better, BEST

If you're a parent, you know that teaching your child to discern between good and bad is complicated enough; teaching them to separate better and best adds even greater complexity. Many people settle for the good presently available to them rather than yearning for what is best. As Christians, we cannot settle for good. We must remember this:

TRUTH #3: The best is yet to be; it's a promise.

A growing number of Christians are looking for their "best life now," almost as if they could establish "their kingdom come" on earth. This is a dangerous lie! Followers of Christ are called to fix their eyes on what is ahead, what is unseen, what is promised by God.

Read 2 Corinthians 4:16–18. When circumstances tempt us to let go in despair, what encouragement can we take from this passage?

_____

_____

If you're looking for your best life now, facing adversity can feel impossible. The best-life-now mentality shrivels quickly in the flames of affliction. The promises of God do not. As powerhouse British preacher and theologian C. H. Spurgeon proclaimed, "The promises of God never shine brighter than in the furnace of affliction."[8]

99

When you're barely holding on, when the fires burn hottest, the promises of God do not merely endure; they shine *even more brilliantly*. The best is yet to come, dear one; that's a promise.

Read 2 Corinthians 5:1–8. In this passage, what promises does God make about life, death, and eternity?

_____

_____

Reread 2 Corinthians 5:7. How might your life look different if you lived by faith in the promises of God rather than by sight?

_____

_____

Rescue at the Red Sea

At times it's hard to see that the best is yet to be, particularly if the present circumstances are overwhelming. Think about the children of Israel. To free them from their Egyptian oppressors, the Lord led the Israelites into the wilderness and then to the shores of the Red Sea. Looking back at the enemy chariots and toward the vast waters, God's people felt trapped. Despite the fact that they had witnessed His mighty power delivering them from ten horrific plagues in Egypt, overcoming an enemy behind and an ocean in front felt impossible.

They cried, "Leave us alone! Let us be slaves to the Egyptians. It's better to be a slave in Egypt than a corpse in the wilderness!" (Exod. 14:12).

If, like the Israelites, we look more intently at our circumstances than we do at our Lord, it's easy to give up hope. When we stop trusting God, our minds can quickly take us to some very dark places. We have a choice, though. We can choose to stand on God's promises, or we can fan the flame of our imagination. Left on our own, it's very easy to lose heart.

The Israelites were losing heart—and quickly!—but in this moment of affliction, the "yet to be" promise of God shone brilliantly: "Don't be afraid. Just stand still and watch the LORD rescue you today" (Exod. 14:13).

And rescue them He did. Mightily. Miraculously. Magnificently.

And rescue *you* He *will*.

He will rescue you mightily.

He will rescue you miraculously.

He will rescue you magnificently.

Read Isaiah 43:16–19. In this passage, the prophet refers to the Israelites being rescued and the Egyptian charioteers being swept away by God's glorious deliverance. What promise does He make about the future yet to be?

_____

_____

Take some moments to be still and silent. Ask the Lord to open the eyes of your heart so you can see the new things He is doing and/or the ways He is making a way in the wilderness. Ask Him to show you how He is currently fighting for you and to reveal any ways He's asking you to stand still and allow Him to fight rather than frantically try to figure things out on your own. Use the space below to respond to Him in prayer.

_____

_____

_____

As we close this final session, allow me to remind you of the ultimate promise yet to be. Read Revelation 21:1–7 and write down the promises of God that will get you all the way home.

_____

_____

Finally, rewrite the three main truths we studied in this session, asking the Holy Spirit to seal them in your heart and mind.

1. _____

2. _____

3. _____

Look at the journey we've taken together. Thank you for your commitment to dive deep into God's Word, to let go of things that may have held you back, and to take a fresh gaze at our glorious Savior. May all you've learned help you more courageously hold on to Jesus when despair tempts you to let go. Above all, may you remember that you are being held by the God of all creation, who loves you more than you can ask for or imagine. I'm entrusting you to Him today.

Notes

Session 1 Holding On When Life Feels Out of Control

1. Sheila Walsh, *Holding On When You Want to Let Go* (Grand Rapids: Baker Books, 2021), 25.

2. Pierre Wolff, *Discernment: The Art of Choosing Well: Based on Ignatian Spirituality*, 2nd ed. (Liguori, MO: Liguori/Triumph, 2003), 120.

Session 2 Holding On When You Feel Alone and God Is Silent

1. "45. agkura," Bible Hub, accessed February 2, 2021, https://biblehub.com/greek/45.htm.

2. "152. aischuné," Bible Hub, accessed February 4, 2021, https://biblehub.com/greek/152 .htm; and "2617. kataischuno," accessed February 4, 2021, https://biblehub.com/greek/2617.htm.

3. Lewis B. Smedes, *Shame and Grace: Healing the Shame We Don't Deserve* (San Francisco: HarperSanFrancisco, 1993), 5.

Session 3 Holding On When You're Afraid

1. Philip Yancey, *What's So Amazing About Grace?* (Grand Rapids: Zondervan, 1997), 45.

2. "Bono: Grace over Karma," *Christianity Today*, August 1, 2005, https://www.christianitytoday .com/ct/2005/augustweb-only/bono-0805.html.

3. Walsh, *Holding On When You Want to Let Go*, 93.

Session 4 Holding On When You've Messed Up

1. "266. hamartia," Bible Hub, accessed February 9, 2021, https://biblehub.com/greek/266.htm; and "264. hamatanó," Bible Hub, accessed February 9, 2021, https://biblehub.com/greek/264.htm.

2. Dictionary.com, s.v. "repentance," accessed February 9, 2021, https://www.dictionary.com /browse/repentance?s=t.

3. John J. Parsons, "Thoughts on Repentance: Teshuva, Metanoia, and Strepho," Hebrew for Christians, accessed February 9, 2021, https://www.hebrew4christians.com/Holidays/Fall_Holi days/Elul/Teshuvah/teshuvah.html.

4. "3341. metanoia," Bible Hub, accessed February 25, 2021, https://biblehub.com/greek/3341.htm.

Session 5 Held by the Promises of God

1. "1459. egkataleipó," Bible Hub, accessed February 10, 2021, https://biblehub.com/greek /1459.htm.

2. Wilfred E. Major and Michael Laughy, "46. The Subjunctive Mood," *Ancient Greek for Everyone*, accessed February 10, 2021, https://ancientgreek.pressbooks.com/chapter/46/.

3. "Aman," Blue Letter Bible, accessed February 18, 2021, https://www.blueletterbible.org/lang/lexicon/lexicon.cfm?t=kjv&strongs=h539.

Session 6 Held by the God Who Rescues

1. William McRaven, "U.S. Ranger Raid on Cabanatuan, 30 January 1945," *Spec Ops: Case Studies in Special Operations Warfare: Theory and Practice*, originally published 1996, accessed February 16, 2021, https://publicism.info/history/spec_ops/7.html.

2. Erin Blakemore, "5 of History's Most Dramatic Rescues," History, updated August 22, 2018, https://www.history.com/news/most-dramatic-rescues-in-history-baby-jessica-chilean-miners-andrea-doria.

3. "5337. natsal," Bible Hub, accessed February 17, 2021, https://biblehub.com/hebrew/5337.htm.

4. "4982. sózó," Bible Hub, accessed February 17, 2021, https://biblehub.com/greek/4982.htm.

5. "4506. rhuomai," Bible Hub, accessed February 17, 2021, https://biblehub.com/greek/4506.htm.

6. "1805. exagorazó," Bible Hub, accessed February 17, 2021, https://biblehub.com/greek/1805.htm.

7. C. S. Lewis, *Mere Christianity* (New York: HarperCollins, 2001), 82.

Session 7 Held by the God of Miracles Who Changes Everything

1. Walsh, *Holding On When You Want to Let Go*, 164.

2. Lewis Smedes, *Forgive and Forget: Healing the Hurts We Don't Deserve* (New York: HarperCollins, 1996), 136–37.

Session 8 Let Go! You Are Being Held

1. Norman Vincent Peale, *The Power of Positive Thinking* (New York: Touchstone, 2015), 153.

2. "4768. stugnazó," Bible Hub, accessed February 21, 2021, https://biblehub.com/greek/4768.htm.

3. Shel Silverstein, *The Missing Piece* (New York: HarperCollins Children's Books, 1976), 1.

4. Richard R. Lingeman, "The Third Mr. Silverstein," *New York Times*, April 30, 1978, https://www.nytimes.com/1978/04/30/archives/the-third-mr-silverstein.html.

5. "James 1:4," Bible Hub, accessed February 21, 2021, https://biblehub.com/text/james/1-4.htm.

6. "3648. holokléros," Bible Hub, accessed February 21, 2021, https://biblehub.com/greek/3648.htm.

7. "5046. teleios," Bible Hub, accessed February 21, 2021, https://biblehub.com/greek/5046.htm.

8. Warren Wiersbe, *The Wiersbe Bible Commentary: Old Testament* (Colorado Springs: David C. Cook, 2007), 88.

SHEILA WALSH grew up in Scotland and has spoken to over six million women around the world. Her passion is being a Bible teacher, making God's Word practical, and sharing her own story of how God met her when she was at her lowest point and lifted her up again. Her message: GOD IS HOLDING YOU! Sheila loves writing and has sold more than five million books. She is also the cohost of the television program *Life Today*, airing in the US, Canada, Europe, and Australia, with a potential audience of over one hundred million viewers daily. Calling Texas home, Sheila lives in Dallas with her husband, Barry, and two little dogs, Tink and Maggie, who rule the roost. Sheila and Barry's son, Christian, is in graduate school in Texas.